The Architecture of
Microcomputers:
Fundamentals

Little, Brown Computer Systems Series

Gerald M. Weinberg, Editor

Weinberg, Gerald M.
  Rethinking Systems Analysis and Design

Weinberg, Gerald M.
  Understanding the Professional Programmer

Weinberg, Gerald M., Stephen E. Wright, Richard Kauffman, and Martin A. Goetz
  High Level COBOL Programming

Windeknecht, Thomas G.
  6502 Systems Programming

The Architecture of Microcomputers
Volume I:
Fundamentals

with revisions

S. E. Greenfield

State University of New York at Albany

Little, Brown and Company

Boston   Toronto

Library of Congress Cataloging in Publication Data

Greenfield, S. E.
  The architecture of microcomputers.

  (Little, Brown computer systems series)
  Contents: v. 1. Fundamentals with revisions.
  1. Computer architecture.   2. Microcomputers.
I. Title.   II. Series.
QA76.9.A73G73 1983   621.3819′52   82-25905
ISBN 0-316-32674-7 (v. 1)

Library of Congress Catalog Card Number 82-25905

ISBN 0-316-32674-7

9 8 7 6 5 4 3 2 1

MV

Published simultaneously in Canada
by Little, Brown & Company (Canada) Limited

Printed in the United States of America

*to Peg, Doug, Randy,
and Janine*

Preface

The underlying theme throughout this book is the communication of *basic* principles of microcomputer architecture. Specifically, it is intended for the student of microcomputer architecture and for the microcomputer user. This has dictated that the coverage of architectural characteristics should not be limited to any particular microcomputer, but rather should be applicable to microcomputers in general.

If the history of microcomputers until now is any criterion, then whatever appears as a contemporary product today will not be a contemporary product two years hence. But the basic principles that have evolved should remain applicable for all microcomputers.

The material contained herein evolved from a combined graduate and undergraduate course in microcomputer architecture. The course was given at the State University of New York at Albany (SUNYA) in the Computer Science Department from 1974 to the present. It was initially designed to be at the graduate level, but was modified to accommodate undergraduates with a sequence in computer science. The students were well versed in the programming techniques required for a major in computer science. They were not engineering students, however, so the course material had to stem from a base of programming knowledge. Because it was a one-semester course, the key criterion had to be relevancy. The course contained only material relevant to microcomputer structures.

Because the microcomputer is merely an evolution of basic computer development, a large storehouse of material on processor architecture has become standard academic fare. Thus, care was required in avoiding traditional but currently insignificant material. Techniques that have become obsolete had to be sifted out to make way for more contemporary thinking. Therefore, the depth of detail in the material presented here is subject to a professional judgment of how relevant the topic is to a basic understanding of the subject. As a result, certain areas are explored in extensive detail, while other material is less embellished. Material from manufacturers has occasionally been included as a supplement *only*, to show the reader what is actually available.

Chapter 1 is a general introduction to microcomputers. It discusses the history and evolution of the subject and gives a general overview of the field. "Chip" technology is discussed at a survey level because this aspect of microcomputers has been changing at a considerable rate.

The basics of logic design are covered in chapter 2. It is a detailed and self-contained treatment of the fundamentals required for dealing with the successive material. If this material is used in a course in which basic logic design is a prerequisite, then chapter 2, and the problems at its end, could serve as a quick review.

In chapter 3, the flip-flop is introduced as a basic digital memory element that can be constructed from NOR elements. An introduction to state diagrams is used in conjunction with Karnaugh maps as the basis of deriving the logic equations for the major types of flip-flops. The use of flip-flops as the basic elements of *registers* is discussed and is used to introduce the computer functions that control the usage of a register (i.e., *shifting*, *counting*, etc.). These functions are developed independently, but the chapter concludes by explaining the techniques of *superimposing* functions used with a single register.

Chapter 4 gives the student a grounding in sequential logic techniques and also introduces the methods used for performing clocked operations. It emphasizes the use of state diagrams to initiate the logic synthesis procedure. Level outputs and pulsed sequential logic à la Mealy/Moore are also covered. The section on *flip-flop conversions* is presented as a systematic means of converting the implementation of one flip-flop format to another (i.e., conversion of SR to T).

This book was initially published in a hardbound version that incorporated Volumes I and II. In Volume I, *Fundamentals*, are contained the techniques necessary as a foundation for understanding the structure of a microcomputer. These basic tools are described and examined in detail.

In Volume II, *Structures*, the fundamental techniques are utilized to explore the actual microcomputer structure. This includes the structural segments, the instructions and their implementation, and the control of operations. These are integrated to describe the microcomputer as an entity.

This book provides a self-contained course for the student who desires to attain a proficiency in microcomputer architecture. As a classroom supplement to this text, a required project was given to the graduate students at SUNYA. The project first necessitated a mutual selection (between instructor and student) of a commercial microprocessor. If possible, a different model was used by each student. Second, the student was required to answer a set of questions on the selected processor's characteristics, including such topics as subroutine mechanisms and interrupt structure. In addition, the generalized structure described in Volume II was used as a reference model, so that the selected processor had to be presented in that format. In this manner, the course material would be related to the student's project. The time spent in extracting the information contained in the manufacturer's manuals worked as a practical reinforcement of basic ideas.

This book contains a certain amount of supplemental material from microcomputer manufacturers. I thank them for their generous consent to my use of the material.

S. E. Greenfield

Contents

Chapter 1

Microcomputers

The subject of microcomputer architecture begins with a process called MOS (Metal Oxide Semiconductor). It is a process for placing many electronic digital circuits onto a miniscule "chip" of silicon—many more circuits, in fact, than have ever before been possible.

Interestingly, the basic concept of MOS goes as far back as the 1930s, when work was done by J. E. Lilienfield. Because of material problems, it was not a practical device at that time. The process continued to evolve, but it was many years before the technologists learned how to use the technology productively. Eventually, in the 1970s, the MOS process reached a level of sophistication where the entire central part of a small computer could be placed on a single chip. This, then, was the birth of the microcomputer!

It is a fantastic development which should have a tremendous impact on our society. Undoubtedly, historians 100 years hence will laud the microcomputer as a particularly significant part of the "computer age." If we consider its effects to date, we see the microcomputer extending existing computer technology into many more aspects of our lives than was ever before possible—because small compact computers are priced under a thousand dollars rather than in the tens of thousands.

Even without the microcomputer, our economic structure has become dependent on computers (see table 1-1). Banking, credit, the stock market, and transportation reservation systems are all slaves to computerized operations. These systems can now give more services while the computer takes on the burden of the multifold increased bookkeeping.

The microcomputer gives us the opportunity to extend computerization into areas where the cost was formerly prohibitive. It is now possible

Table 1-1 Microcomputer Applications—Anywhere That Something Has to Be Done in Response to an Input

Input	Output	Application
Thermostat temperature	Furnace switch	Heating control
"	Motor switch	Air conditioning control
Keyboard	Printer signal	Typewriter control
Keyboard	Data on tape	Cash register
Timing	Switch control	Traffic lights
Switch (or knob)	TV display	TV games
Sensors	Engine timing	Automotive

2

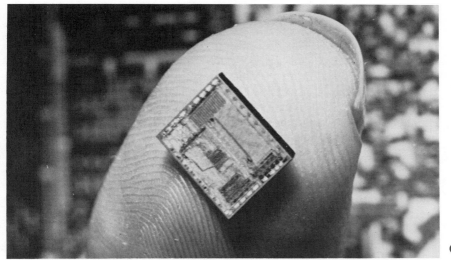

Figure 1-1 (a) Unpackaged Microprocessor Chip. (b) Packaged Microprocessor with Wafer. (Courtesy Intel Corporation)

for the smallest businesses to profitably use microcomputers. These small inexpensive systems can assume such fundamental tasks as inventory control, the generation of customer mailing lists, and many ledger functions. Larger businesses will also find systems useful in reducing the cost of equipment used in production processes, even to the extent of using a small computer at each piece of machinery. Also, medical instrumentation and monitoring equipment are now using microcomputers.

Such consumer items as microcomputer games are now a reality and are available at neighborhood department stores. In addition, automobiles now contain microcomputers to control timing and many other under-the-hood functions. Credit card shopping is aided by microcomputerized cash registers that communicate instant credit verification.

These are all aspects of computerized operations which evolved from earlier applications of both "monster" computers and "mini" computers. The inexpensive "micro" computer has made computerized operations economically feasible with much smaller equipment.

The individual, too, can be more personally involved because a microcomputer can potentially be used anywhere for automatically controlling functions in the home. Personal computing magazines have sprung up to satisfy the needs of individual users. In the spiraling complexity of our society, even more complexity is offered to the individuals who want to learn the intricacies of programming. They have within their economic reach the hardware to run their own computer programs. The applications can range from simplistic hobbies to real utility. It's a gadgeteer's dream world.

Household applications include microcomputer control of the timing of home heating and air conditioning systems. A programmed sequence might monitor such tasks as the shopping lists for a week, a month, or a year. The household budget can be programmed onto a Read Only Memory chip of silicon, so that daily spending habits can be religiously monitored by the computer.

Where this will end is only conjecture, but there is no doubt that the microcomputer is working itself into our daily lives. The microcomputer will become at least as much a part of our society as has the small electronic calculator in an unbelievably short time.

1.1 WHERE THE COMPUTER BEGAN

Humans have always attempted to ease the burden of computation. The abacus was an early development which has not disappeared even at this late date. The slide rule was popular with engineers until the very recent emergence of inexpensive electronic calculators—one of the early results

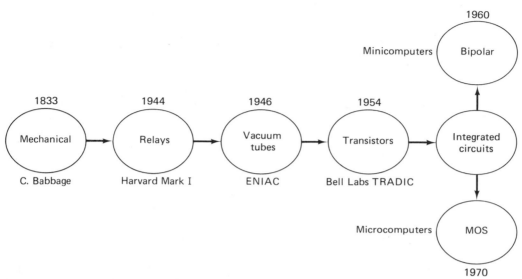

Figure 1-2   Computer Technology Evolution

of MOS. In fact, they were a proving ground for the feasibility of MOS technology in microcomputers.

Very early in our history, the search began for a means to perform automatic computation. In figure 1-2, the evolution of technology for computers is traced. In 1833, Charles Babbage proposed a mechanically driven computer which had all the elements of a modern computer: control, arithmetic, and memory. However, the task was too immense for the technology of the day, and the machine was never completed.

It wasn't until this century, when electronic components became available, that a real breakthrough was made. In 1944, electromechanical relays were used to make the earliest "monster" computers, the Harvard Mark I and II. The Mark I was actually more mechanical than the Mark II, which made more extensive use of relays. Although these machines were really more programmable calculators rather than computers, their ponderous presence (the Mark I was 50 feet long) was quite impressive.

The implications of their potential were quite frightening to some writers of that time; many predicted that this type of "brain" could somehow take over our society. They would be in a state of paralysis if they could have looked ahead thirty years to see grade school children using $10 electronic calculators to do their homework or, more significantly, the availability of the much more efficient microcomputers of today.

Historically, it is interesting to note that even the Aiken Mark I at Harvard was preceded by the development of the German Zuse computer (Z3) in 1941. This work was performed independently, but because of the war there was no communication of ideas.

The first electronic computer was built in 1946, using 18,000 vacuum tubes. This was the ENIAC, and it was the beginning of a chain of electronic computers. Each in turn was followed by further improvements in electronic technology (see figure 1-3).

The most significant contribution occurred in 1946, with the publication of a paper by John Von Neumann. He proposed the architecture for a stored program computer, which in its genius has become the model for all present-day computers. Significantly tied to the stored program idea was his proposal that a computer memory could be used either for instructions or for data. The methodology for distinguishing between these two was simply the ability to know when one or the other was being used.

The development of the transistor in 1948 marked a new era in electronics in which more compact, solid-state circuits emerged at a time when our society was rushing headlong into a vacuum tube dependency. The first transistorized digital computer, the TRADIC, was built at Bell Laboratories in 1954. It was followed by a gradual conversion of computers to transistorization.

The evolution of transistors to integrated circuits was very significant in that it allowed quicker development of new computer architecture, each offering more efficiency and cleverness than its predecessors. The bipolar integrated circuits blossomed in the 1960s and acted as a catalyst to the minicomputer. The mini, the smallest computer of its time, offered a way of placing a monster computer's capability into applications with smaller requirements and even smaller budgets.

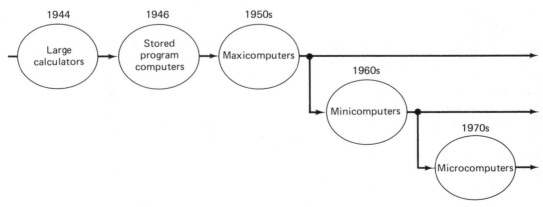

Figure 1-3 Microcomputer Evolution

These advances now allowed a computer to be used in such operations as the inventory of machinery parts in a factory or for setting up a small computation center where every second of computer time did not have to be charged to pay the rent on the computer.

1.2 THE FIRST MICROCOMPUTERS

When a technology is evolutionary, rather than revolutionary, it requires some research to assign proper credit for firsts. Where was the first microcomputer designed and built? It actually came about because of a very ambitious undertaking in 1968. A group of scientists and engineers at the Mitre Corporation, in Bedford, Massachusetts, felt that MOS technology had evolved to the point where it was ready for transition to the real world.

A company called Viatron was established, which ambitiously hoped to force a data-processing revolution. It contended that the high circuit density and relative inexpensiveness of MOS was a natural for developing very inexpensive data terminals and computers. Viatron conceived of terminals, used by clerks, renting for $39 a month that could replace the expensive terminals then in use.

The heart of the terminal was an inexpensive MOS microprocessor which added intelligence to the terminal. Viatron also developed the 2140, which was presumably the first MOS computer in this country designed around an MOS microprocessor. The technology used was PMOS silicon gate.

This microprocessor was basically a 4-bit slice that could expand into a computer of any word size. This computer, which rented for $99 a month, could collect and concentrate the data from many terminals at one site and then transmit the data to a central "monster" computer. It could also be a stand-alone MOS microcomputer.

To build these two MOS microcomputers, and all the additional circuitry required, meant that Viatron needed more MOS production capability than then existed in the United States. Up to then, the only available MOS capability was geared to a calculator market that had not yet matured.

The economic impact that Viatron proposed was such that the supporting semiconductor companies felt that Viatron's presence could not be ignored. The result was a tooling-up to support the orders for MOS circuits placed by Viatron. If Viatron was not successful, these companies reasoned, then they could always hedge their bets by entering the calculator market. Thus, the MOS production stampede was initiated.

Viatron made about 2,000 systems before the economic downfall of 1970 had its effect and Viatron went under. But the MOS momentum was still there. Efforts were shifted to the burgeoning calculator market. This meant that much more attention had to be given to MOS technology by semiconductor makers.

It was inevitable that the designers of calculators would also consider the possibility of a small computer on a chip. In 1970, Intel Company engineers in Santa Clara, California, initiated a new effort taking a calculator design and extending it to operate as a small stored-program computer using PMOS technology. This evolved into the Intel 4004 chip, which was the CPU for a 4-bit computer which was introduced in 1971 to control a small printing calculator.

Although it required a collection of support chips to perform any computer functions, it was nevertheless a computer on a chip. Over 2,000 transistors were microminiaturized on this chip. Although the initial market reaction was not that strong, nevertheless the potential for micro-computers began to look more promising.

Companies such as Rockwell, National, and Fairchild introduced microprocessors to the market with sufficient acceptance to encourage further activity. Intel followed the 4004 with the 8008, an 8-bit processor with limited speed capabilities. In 1974, the modern microprocessor began. Intel announced the 8080 microcomputer, which used the faster NMOS technology. Also, the architecture of the 8080 had more capability than prior microcomputers.

Table 1-2   Microprocessor Historical Development

Year	Company	Development
1968	Viatron Computer	Developed first 8-bit LSI microprocessor used to control a data terminal
1969	Viatron Computer	Developed first 4-bit LSI microprocessor used as basic element in a minicomputer
1971	Intel	Developed 4-bit 4004 for commercial sales
1972	Rockwell Fairchild Intel	PPS-4 microprocessor PPS-25 microprocessor 8008
1973	National Intel	IMP 8080
1974	Motorola Monolithic Memories	6800 Bit-slice introduction
1975	TI Fairchild	4-bit slice F-8

It was followed a year later by Motorola's 6800, which had such features as index registers, two accumulators, and an input-output system that looked like memory.

The next step, the entry by other semiconductor companies with their microcomputer designs, was quite predictable. The microcomputer had arrived (see table 1-2).

1.3 THE TECHNOLOGY

The MOS circuitry, the basis for the microcomputer chip, is part of the overall family of integrated circuits. Integrated circuits became available in the early 1960s, when the silicon planar technique was developed, in which an insulating layer of oxide was grown and etched on a silicon substrate. The first circuits contained a small collection of logic gates on one chip. The earliest interest came from digital circuit designers who were excited at the possibility of more logic gates in a smaller area and at less cost.

As these integrated circuits became more readily available, they began to work into computer hardware. In fact, the integrated circuit was the biggest boost to the evolution of the minicomputer in the late 1960s. The ultimate goal was to have more and more circuits on one chip so that large-scale integration (LSI) could be achieved. As the quest continued, the earlier integrated circuits, with up to a dozen gates in a chip, were in retrospect named small-scale integration (SSI). The achievement of a counter on a chip, or a 4- or 8-bit register which used up to 100 gates, although not LSI was certainly an advancement. These intermediate devices were labeled medium-scale integration, or MSI.

In figure 1-4, the transition from SSI to LSI is shown. Figures 1-5 through 1-8 show a package and these circuits in more detail. Except for the MOS/LSI case, all the others use a bipolar technology. The bipolar has much faster circuitry, ideal for fast minicomputers, but lacks the ability to place over 3,000 transistors on one substrate. The bipolar process requires that the carrier flows through the bulk of the material, so that a significant isolation of devices is necessary.

The MOS chip (see figure 1-9) operates on a field effect principle in which carriers operate on the surface of the material. The MOS device has a tremendous real estate density advantage, but lacks the speed of the bipolar devices. Figure 1-2 shows that LSI has also been obtained to a certain extent with bipolar devices. This is the implementation for most bit slice designs.

The real progress in MOS depended on a process called *photolithography*, which produced photomasks of each layer of processing. These masks had to have high resolution and high-dimensional contact.

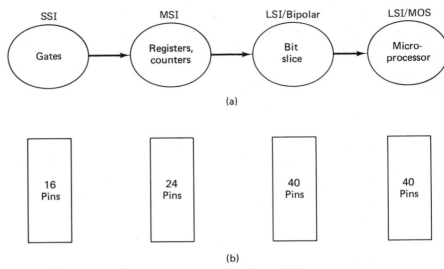

(a)

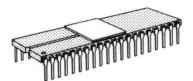

(b)

Figure 1-4   Integrated Circuits (a) and Packages (b)

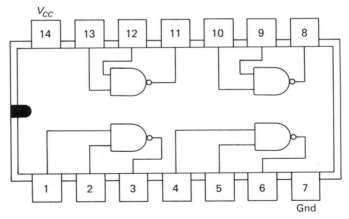

Figure 1-5   The Microprocessor Package

Figure 1-6   SSI Integrated Circuit

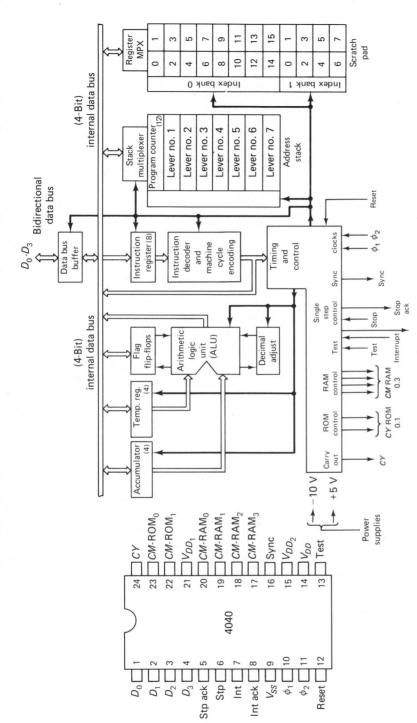

Figure 1-7 LSI Integrated Circuit (Intel 4040 Microprocessor)

11

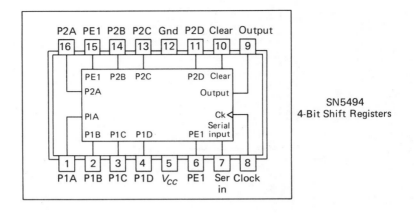

SN5494
4-Bit Shift Registers

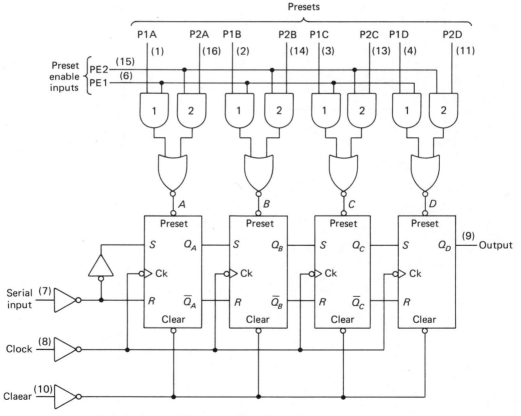

Figure 1-8   MSI Integrated Circuit

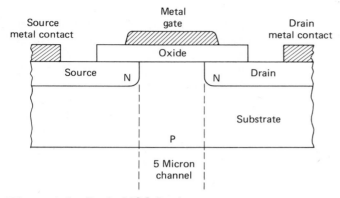

Figure 1-9 Basic MOS Device

The actual technique for constructing an integrated circuit (IC) follows this procedure:

1. Develop a logic diagram which describes the circuit, and assign pins to input and output.
2. Convert each logic circuit to a "device" which performs the logic.
3. Develop a master drawing (or mask) for each layer which will be processed on a silicon surface to make the IC.

    Each layer is either adding conductive paths (thin film deposition) of material such as aluminum or is diffusing an area on the silicon to develop the circuit (bipolar technology is different in that it injects impurities into the device).
4. By photolithography, transfer the masks to the silicon surface.
5. After all layers are inscribed on the surface, the integrated circuit process is obtained.

Table 1-3 MOS Technology

Technology	Gate Delay (nanoseconds)	Gate Density (gates/mm²)
P Channel (metal gate)	80	50
P Channel (silicon gate)	30	90
N Channel (silicon gate)	10	95
CMOS (silicon gate)	10	45
CMOS (SOS)	3	100
Schottkey Bipolar	6	25
I²L (integrated injection logic)	50	40

The many MOS techniques being explored for potential microcomputer applications are summarized in table 1-3. The P channel MOS was the earliest process used. In the search for a faster process, N channel evolved. A complementary technique using both P and N channels is called CMOS. Its greatest advantage is a very low power drain. Its relative disadvantage is that it requires more area than NMOS.

Techniques for eliminating disadvantages and effecting improvements are continuously occurring—such as CMOS/SOS. SOS, which means "silicon on sapphire," is a method of speeding up a CMOS circuit, so that the natural low power characteristic of CMOS can be combined with higher speed operation.

1.4 WHAT IS A MICROCOMPUTER?

Basically, the microcomputer is not very different from a minicomputer, except that it may have less of a variety of instructions, a smaller word size, and perform at slower speeds. This statement suggests that the microcomputer is merely a reduced-capability minicomputer. Functionally, this is very much the case, but physically there is an additional distinction. Because a large portion of the central computing elements can be placed on an MOS chip, the potential for a computer system with significantly reduced cost becomes a major factor. In other words, the microcomputer can do many jobs that require computer performance in which the minicomputer is just too much machine for the job.

Prior to the microcomputer, a management decision process often traded off a $10,000 minicomputer against a machine that could be specifically designed for the job. A factor to be considered in addition to the product cost was the time required to generate the new design. This time, in turn, had to be compared with the time and cost in programming and maintaining a minicomputer. All too often, the special design could be produced at a cost significantly below that of the minicomputer. This occurred most often in "dedicated" applications, in which the computer was performing a specific task rather than performing general computations—for example, the control of the operation of automatic machinery, of data display equipment, or communications equipment.

Whenever many units were required, the initial cost of design of a dedicated controller could be amortized over the number of units to be produced. However, when very few units or even a single unit were required, the minicomputer was the only possible answer to avoid the excessive cost of tooling for a special design. With the availability of microcomputers, many special purpose designs were easily replaced without requiring new hardware, simply by programming the problem. In addition, this could often be done much less expensively than before.

Whenever a microcomputer is not chosen to replace special-purpose logic, it is more than likely because of requirements for higher speeds that could not be obtained from a microcomputer.

Thus, microcomputers are now used in applications where either available computers were not formerly used because of cost or performance or both; or minicomputers were being used but are now replaced by the less expensive microcomputers.

1.5 THE MICROPROCESSOR SYSTEM

The microcomputer as a system has as its basis the microprocessor chip. These chips come in various sizes and are implemented in various technologies. When the micro*processor* chips are combined with other integrated circuits, a micro*computer* system can be constructed. The majority of these have been 8-bit data-oriented, although the number of 16-bit devices is increasing.

In addition to these processors, devices called "bit slices" are also available. These are usually not self-contained microprocessors. They are "super MSI" bipolar chips with portions of CPU logic that allow the users to define their own architecture. This device is used quite extensively as a key element in minicomputers, often using the very popular 2901 4-bit wide bit slice element. A system using bit slices is shown in figure 1-10.

One of the continually evolving aspects of the physical microcomputer system topology is the amount of functions centered on a single chip. Most LSI chips now available are really microprocessors. To qualify as a microcomputer requires the addition of enough circuits to allow basic computer functions to take place—usually a basic arithmetic processor that can interact with a memory and also control the input and output of data.

Some microcomputers for limited applications are self-contained on a single chip. For example, the Intel 8748 contains 64 words of data

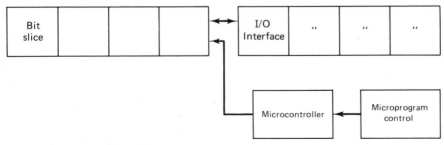

Figure 1-10   LSI Bit Slice

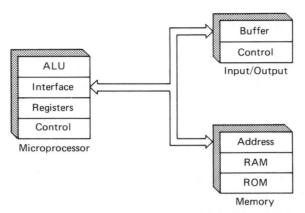

Figure 1-11   The Main Elements of a Microprocessor

memory, 1024 words of fixed-program memory, an oscillator, and some input/output control. Such units are useful for applications that do not require extensive computation, but do demand minimum physical space. Undoubtedly, the technology will eventually permit more capability in the single chip package.

The following is an outline of the basic functions which make up a microcomputer (see figure 1-11).

The *microprocessor* function contains four basic sections:
1. ALU—the arithmetic logic unit
2. INTERFACING
3. CONTROL
4. REGISTERS

The *memory* contains three basic sections:
1. RAM—random access memory
2. ROM—optional read-only memory
3. ADDRESS—memory address register

The *input/output* (I/O) control contains two basic sections:
1. BUFFERING
2. CONTROL—I/O sequencing and priority logic.

Each of these elements is discussed briefly for the purpose of developing a better feeling for the parts which make up a microprocessor.

The Microprocessor

The microprocessor itself is usually a partitioning of the processor function into one or more chips. These functions are performed in a manner similar to the central processor of a larger computer.

1. ALU The arithmetic logic unit is the central element in the entire microcomputer. A typical implementation of the ALU function includes primitive arithmetic operations such as the addition and subtraction of data words. The unit also performs logic operations such as "and," "or," and "exclusive or." Quite often, the majority of the miscellaneous processor operations, such as register counting, will all be centralized here. This is advantageous, because the ALU already contains the basic logic pieces used to perform most operations.

2. Interfacing This is a key problem area in a microprocessor. It must face the question of how to handle the interaction between functions on different chips and, more specifically, the interfacing of the processor functions with the memory and the input/output. An obvious answer to one aspect, the interaction of processor functions, is the emergence of true single-chip processors.

In the first-generation chips (such as the Intel 4004), additional logic was required to interface the various microprocessor pieces, such as the timing and the interfaces to memory and input/output (figure 1-12). Because of the problems in adjusting timing circuits, it was quite common to have an external clock. In some of the later microprocessors the timing was placed on the chip itself (figure 1-13). The only external connection required was a crystal oscillator.

As the chips evolved, memory addressing was assigned to separate pins to eliminate some of the memory interface requirements (figure 1-14). This had certain limitations, because the amount of memory circuits that could be electrically driven from MOS was small—if the memory requirements were extensive, then additional "driving" circuits were still required.

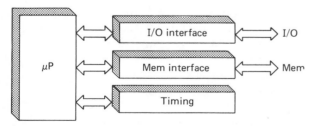

Figure 1-12   Early Configuration with Support Elements

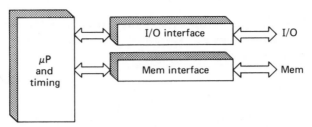

Figure 1-13   Configuration with Integrated Clock

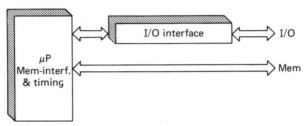

Figure 1-14

3. Control The microcontrol area is where the sequencing of the CPU is controlled and the interaction with memory and I/O is scheduled. Some microprocessors use random logic and place the control on the same chip as the ALU (8080, 6800), which, of course, requires more logic functions on the chip. The decision of how to best partition the functions is significantly dependent on how the control is implemented.

When using a full microcoded control, it is often desirable to separate the control function from the other processor functions. This is because the ROM can now be implemented by any standard commercial ROM chip, and thus the CPU chip becomes less dense with a potentially higher yield (figure 1-15). This technique is used in the Digital LSI-11. It results in additional chips which are used to microprogram the microprocessor. The flexibility of added functions obtained from the microprogrammed technique will quite often offset the cost of the additional control chips. In fact, the additional chips necessary to add functions to nonmicroprogrammed processors will often add more chips to the system than required for microprogrammed control.

This fact indicates that the assignments of functions to a chip are not always done with total system minimization as a goal. Further, there is a preoccupation by the manufacturer to present the "one-chip" microprocessor. This is, of course, quite desirable for controller applications. But when used in a *systems* application, the resulting large chip count often comes as a shock and is a reminder of the meaning of *caveat emptor*.

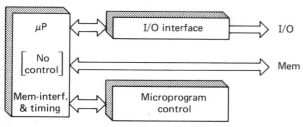

Figure 1-15 Microprogrammed Control

4. Registers The register section of the CPU varies considerably from processor to processor. The number of registers may vary from 1 to 64. Some of the possible uses of the registers are for address modification, for saving subroutine addresses, for the program counter, for auxiliary accumulators, or as a small scratch pad memory. Of course, various combinations of these uses depend on the architectural plan.

The Memory

The interfacing of the processor with memory requires some amount of read/write memory, which is usually random access (RAM). Portions of this can be replaced by a fixed program in read-only memory (ROM). For systems with large amounts of memory, a *memory address register* must be added. Some processor chips do not have sufficient logic to handle the expansion of memory, so that additional external control circuitry is necessary.

The Input/Output

The I/O control section is always the most difficult portion of the computer to standardize. But, in general, *buffering* of data and control is almost always required between I/O devices and the computer. The effort to place as much of this as possible on the processor chip is a continuing effort.

The proper sequencing of I/O data to and from the processor demands that some of this *control* be incorporated into the microcontrol of the processor. However, this may not be sufficient if there is any expansion of I/O functions, so that additional control with additional circuits will likely be needed.

The Microcomputer System

When all the pieces are put together to form a usable microcomputer, no matter how the manufacturer partitioned the "computer-on-a-chip," it has become a "computer-on-a-board." How well the pieces intermesh to form a smoothly functioning computer structure will determine the success of the architectural plan.

1.6 CONTEMPORARY MICROCOMPUTERS

Examination of the more recently emerging microcomputers suggests that there have been two developmental phases.

During the first phase, from 1976 to 1980, the 8-bit microcomputer became an accepted part of our culture. Specifically, four processor chips became the basis for a variety of uses. These were:

1. *The Intel 8080.* This widely used chip also spawned some variations that incorporated additional capability on the same chip. Specifically, the 8048 was an 8080 that included Input/Output, Random Access Memory, and Read Only Memory on one chip. Although the extent of these on-chip additions was definitely limited, they were advantageous for small control applications. Another variation was the 8748, in which Programmable Read Only Memory was added.

Significantly, the use of chips such as the 8080 forced the development of a new software industry to satisfy the need for support software not immediately forthcoming from the chip manufacturers.

2. *The Zilog Z80.* First introduced in 1976, this chip was an extension of the 8080 architecture and instruction set. It garnered a very extensive following and has been widely used in personal computers.

3. *The Motorola 6800.* This architecture incorporated an indexing capability, in addition to being one of the first processor chips to use a single voltage source. (.5 volts). Although introduced after the 8080, it developed a large user base.

4. *The 6502* has been manufactured in large quantities and used in many control applications, particularly in data terminals. It has also been used in personal computers, such as the APPLE and the PET.

Although other chips held market position for varying time spans, the above four were most popularly used at the end of the decade.

The second phase appeared around 1979, and extends to the time of publication. This is marked by the shifting of classical minicomputer architecture into the realm of microcomputer chips. These are mostly 16-bit structures, but in some cases are as extensive as 32 bits.

Prior to 1979 there were some initial efforts to generate enthusiasm for 16-bit chips. In 1973 National introduced the Imp-16, which was a 10 microsecond instruction time PMOS microprocessor. They followed this with a bipolar version. General Instrument also introduced a 16-bit chip, the

CP1600. However, it was not until the end of the 70s that the 16-bit architectures began to receive serious attention from the majority of semiconductor manufacturers. By then chip processing technology had progressed so that 16-bit chips had become less expensive.

The result was that almost every manufacturer of 8-bit chips entered into 16-bit processor development. Interestingly, these 16-bit chips have found two distinct areas of application.

The first has been in the areas where they directly compete with their 8-bit predecessors. The 16-bitters have been only slightly more expensive than the 8-bitters, but offer a significant increase in computing power. In fact, some 16-bitters have been repackaged to operate as an 8-bit version of the 16-bitter, for example, the 8088, which is based on the 16-bit Intel 8086. Another variation is to provide an external 8-bit bus to interface with a 16-bit chip, as in the 9995, which is based on the TI 9900. In one case, a basic 8-bitter was enhanced to include more 16-bit functions—the 6809, which is an expansion of Motorola's 8-bit 6800.

The second area of application is much more dramatic. This involves using 16-bit chips in a system that competes directly with 16-bit minicomputers. New companies have developed to provide the software support and the necessary peripherals required for a minicomputer capability.

Table 1-4 presents the most recent entries at the time of publication.

Table 1-4

Microprocessor	Bit Size	Manufacturer
68000	16 (32-bit internal)	Motorola
8086	16	Intel
Z8000	16	Zilog
9900	16	TI
LSI-11	16	DEC
Micronova	32	Data General
16000	16 (32-bit internal)	National
Microvax	32	DEC

The architecture of some of these chips contains extraordinary capabilities. A chip such as the 68000 has 17 CPU registers, each 32-bits wide, which operate on 16-bit data paths. The chip is made up of 70,000 devices! Others, such as the LSI-11 and the Micronova are monolithic chip versions of minicomputers that enjoyed prior market success. The Microvax, being developed for 1984, will place a successful 32-bit architecture into the arena.

Most of these processors will operate with memory management. Almost all will use operating systems such as UNIX. Many personal computer systems are being converted from 8-bit to 16-bit CPUs.

What this means is that the microcomputer will, in the next few years, include that entire class of machines called minicomputers. The only difference will be one of system size, such as the amount and capacity of peripherals, for example, disc storage.

Chapter 2

The Basics of Computer Logic

The architecture of digital computers, more specifically the architecture of microcomputers, uses a design technique which is basic to the structure of any digital machine. This is the technique of digital logic, which includes the mathematics of Boolean algebra, the technique for generating Boolean equations, the topology and interaction of logic circuits, and the methods of minimizing logic equations.

Each subject has been extensively covered in the literature. The presentation here, although not overly lengthy, is reasonably complete for the purpose of understanding the basics of microcomputer architecture.

The discussion of electronic circuits emphasizes the logic function of the circuit rather than the electronics. Thus, an electronics background is not necessary for this part of the material to be both readable and tutorial.

2.1 BOOLEAN ALGEBRA

Of all the tools necessary to analyze and describe the logic of digital computers, Boolean algebra is the most fundamental. For any computer, Boolean equations will describe the operation of the machine in a manner which is independent of the circuit implementation.

The origins of Boolean algebra stem from the work of George Boole, who in 1854 published "An Investigation of the Law of Thought." The application of Boolean algebra to switching circuits was shown in 1938 by Claude Shannon in "Symbolic Analysis of Relay and Switching Circuits."

The following preliminary definitions will facilitate the subsequent discussions.

1. A Boolean variable A can take on only two valuations, 1 or 0, which also have the logical interpretation of true for 1 and false for 0.
2. (a) The operations on a Boolean variable are $\cdot$, $+$, and $-$.
   (b) These operations can be *interpreted* by the English connectives: AND ($\cdot$), OR ($+$), and NOT ($-$).
3. Boolean equations are formed from Boolean variables linked by Boolean operators. For example:

   $F = A \cdot B + B(C + D)$

   (Note: The Boolean multiplication operation $A \cdot B$ can be written as AB, as in conventional algebra.)
4. Boolean algebra is an algebra for manipulating Boolean equations.

24

Interpretations

Although Boolean algebra functions under specific mathematical rules, it is particularly fascinating because it has various other interpretations. The most significant of these are the following:

1. A truth calculus
2. A switching algebra
3. A set theory or algebra of classes

Table 2-1 shows the various interpretations of Boolean operators.

Table 2-1   Interpretations of Boolean Operators

Boolean Operation	Truth Calculus		Switching Algebra	Set Theory (Algebra of Classes)	
·	$\wedge$	AND	Series circuit	$\cap$	Intersection
+	$\vee$	OR	Parallel circuit	$\cup$	Union
0	F	FALSE	Open circuit	$S(Z)$	Null set
1	T	TRUE	Short circuit	$S(U)$	Universal set
$\overline{A}$	$\sim A$	NOT A	Normally closed switch	$C(S)$	Complemented set

1. The *truth calculus* interpretation is a manifestation of symbolic logic, which is a symbolic means of logically describing very simplistic events.

For instance, in a group of three people, Bill, Dick, and Jane, the symbolism B = Bill, D = Dick, and J = Jane can be assigned. Using the notation from table 2-1 for the English connectives, $\wedge$ = AND, $\vee$ = OR, and $\sim$ = NOT, then the following statements can be made:

(a) If Bill and Dick are boys and Jane is a girl, then it is true that the presence of all boys in the group can be described as

Boys = $B \wedge D \wedge (\sim J)$

(b) If an event allows any boy to be present, but excludes the presence of girls, then the participants in the event are described as

Event $= (B \lor D) \land (\sim J)$

(c) An interviewer will talk to any one boy or girl, but if there are two or more individuals present, the interview will not be allowed. This event can be described by a statement of when the interview will *not* occur.

$\sim$Interview $= (B \land D) \lor (D \land J) \lor (J \land B) \lor (B \land D \land J) \lor (\sim B \land \sim D \land \sim J)$

In each case, the English connectives are used to describe the truth or falseness of an event. When this interpretation is applied to a Boolean algebraic expression, it adds a significant dimension of understanding to the mathematical expression.

2. A *switching algebra* offers another way to interpret Boolean algebra. For instance, the Boolean expression $\{A + B\}$ is algebraically A plus B but can be interpreted as a parallel circuit (as in figure 2-1) with two normally open switches A and B. This circuit allows current to pass from point 1 to point 2 if switch A OR B is closed.

In this case, the expression $\{A + B\}$ is interpreted as $\{A \text{ parallel to } B\}$. It should also be obvious that the use of the English connective OR makes $\{A \text{ or } B\}$ an equally effective interpretation.

The Boolean multiplication operation $\{A \cdot B\}$ can be shown to be $\{A \text{ in series with } B\}$ in which current is transmitted (in figure 2-2) from 1 to 2 if both A AND B are closed.

In section 2.3, the use of switching algebra will be examined when switching circuits are examined as a descriptive model.

3. *Set theory* gives an interpretation of Boolean algebra in which the emphasis is on the presence or absence of elements in the set. For a set containing two elements (A, B), the $\{A + B\}$ operation is interpreted as

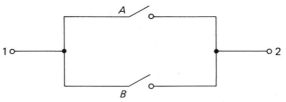

Figure 2-1

Figure 2-2

$\{A \cup B\}$, in which either A alone, B alone, or A and B together form the "union" of A with B.

The Boolean $A \cdot B$ operation in a set theory interpretation becomes A *intersecting* B $\{A \cap B\}$ in which the "intersection" operator selects from a set of elements (A, B) those elements which are contained in both A AND B. In the later discussion of Venn diagrams the use of a diagramatic set theory model will be shown.

2.2 POSTULATES

To define a Boolean algebra, we introduce a set of postulates that will serve as a formal foundation for its use. These postulates will hold for a Boolean algebra that is also interpreted as a truth calculus or a set theory algebra of classes.

Basic List of Postulates for Boolean Algebra

1. X, Y, and Z are elements of the set S.
2. Equivalence is defined for the set S such that

   if $X = Y, Y = Z$

   then $X = Z$

3. The operations $+$, $\cdot$ are defined such that

   $X + Y$ and $X \cdot Y$ are in S

4. All elements in S will take on the valuation

   $S = (0, 1)$

5. For all elements in S, the bar operator will form an element $\overline{X}$ such that when $X = 0$, then $\overline{X} = 1$. This results in the following property:

   $X \cdot \overline{X} = 0$

   $X + \overline{X} = 1$

6. The value 0 has the property that

   $X + 0 = X$

   $X \cdot 0 = 0$

7. The value 1 has the property that

$$X + 1 = 1$$

$$X \cdot 1 = X$$

8. A variable operating on itself has the property that

$$X + X = X$$

$$X \cdot X = X$$

9. The commutative law holds that

$$X + Y = Y + X$$

$$X \cdot Y = Y \cdot X$$

10. The distributive law holds that

$$X \cdot (Y + Z) = (X \cdot Y) + (X \cdot Z)$$

$$X + (Y \cdot Z) = (X + Y) \cdot (X + Z)$$

11. Duality holds that for any identity, if 1 and 0 are interchanged, and also $\cdot$ and $+$ are interchanged, the resulting expression will be a valid dual. For example, given the following:

$$X + \overline{X} = 1, \quad \text{the dual is}$$

$$X \cdot \overline{X} = 0$$

It is interesting to compare Boolean algebra with the normal algebra with which we are most familiar. Most important is that Boolean algebra cannot be expected to perform as in a normal linear algebra. For example, division is not defined as an operation. To operate with a two-valued variable and maintain linear operations, a modulo 2 algebra is required, which does not perform in a logic mode as is done in Boolean algebra.

Also, the $\overline{A}$ operation is not defined in linear algebra. Insofar as the $\cdot$ and $+$ connectives are used, these perform as in ordinary algebra except for the use of $1 + 1 = 1$.

For those interested in examining multivalued nonlinear algebras (as opposed to modulo n linear algebra), the work of E. Post with Post algebra is an excellent starting point.

Basic Theorems

The following theorems are useful in working with Boolean algebra. They can all be proved by using rules and postulates outlined in the previous section.

Theorems of Boolean Algebra

1. $XY + X\overline{Y} = X$
2. $X + XY = X$
3. $X + \overline{X}Y = X + Y$
4. $(X + Y)(\overline{X} + \overline{Y}) = X\overline{Y} + \overline{X}Y$
5. $XY + YZ + Z\overline{X} = XY + Z\overline{X}$ ✓
6. $(X + Y)(\overline{X} + Z) = XZ + \overline{X}Y$ ✓
7. $(X + Y)(\overline{X} + Y) = Y$
8. $(X + Y)(X + \overline{Y}) = X$
9. $XY + XZ = X(Y + Z)$
10. *De Morgan's theorem*

$$F(X, Y, Z, +, \cdot) = \overline{F(\overline{X}, \overline{Y}, \overline{Z}, \cdot, +)}$$

that is,

$$(X + Y + Z) = \overline{(\overline{X} \cdot \overline{Y} \cdot \overline{Z})}$$

also,

$$(X \cdot Y \cdot Z) = \overline{(\overline{X} + \overline{Y} + \overline{Z})}$$

11. *Expansion theorem* for the general sum of products form:

$$F(X, Y, Z) = X \cdot F(1, Y, Z) + \overline{X} \cdot F(0, Y, Z)$$

Expansion theorem for the general product of sums form:

$$F(X, Y, Z) = [X + F(0, Y, Z)] \cdot [\overline{X} + F(1, Y, Z)]$$

The following examples show how the postulates can be used to prove the theorems:

EXAMPLE 2.1

To prove theorem 1

1. Given $XY + X\overline{Y} = X$
2. $X(Y + \overline{Y}) = X$ (Post. 10)
3. $X(1) = X$ (Post. 5)
4. $X = X$ (Post. 7)

EXAMPLE 2.2

To prove theorem 2

1. Given $X + XY = X$
2. $X(1 + Y) = X$ (Post. 10)
3. $X(1) = X$ (Post. 7)
4. $X = X$ (Post. 7)

EXAMPLE 2.3

To prove theorem 3

1. Given $X + \overline{X}Y = X + Y$
2. $X \cdot 1 + \overline{X}Y = X + Y$ (Post. 7)
3. $X(Y + \overline{Y}) + \overline{X}Y = X + Y$ (Post. 5)
4. $XY + X\overline{Y} + \overline{X}Y = X + Y$ (Post. 10)
5. $(XY + XY) + (X\overline{Y} + \overline{X}Y) = X + Y$ (Post. 8)
6. $XY + X\overline{Y} + XY + \overline{X}Y = X + Y$ (Post. 9)
7. $X(Y + \overline{Y}) + Y(X + \overline{X}) = X + Y$ (Post. 10)
8. $X \cdot 1 + Y \cdot 1 = X + Y$ (Post. 5)
9. $X + Y = X + Y$ (Post. 7)

EXAMPLE 2.4

To prove theorem 4

1. Given $(X + Y)(\overline{X} + \overline{Y}) = X\overline{Y} + \overline{X}Y$
2. $X\overline{X} + X\overline{Y} + \overline{X}Y + Y\overline{Y} = X\overline{Y} + \overline{X}Y$ (Post. 10)
3. $0 + X\overline{Y} + \overline{X}Y + 0 = X\overline{Y} + \overline{X}Y$ (Post. 5)
4. $X\overline{Y} + \overline{X}Y = X\overline{Y} + \overline{X}Y$ (Post. 7)

De Morgan's Theorem

Of all the theorems, De Morgan's theorem (theorem 10) has the most significance in that it is a technique for substituting AND operators for OR and vice versa. For example, the logic function $A + B$, when subjected to De Morgan's theorem, forms the equality $A + B = \overline{A} \cdot \overline{B}$. Note that this is not a dual operation, because the placing of the negate bar over a function modified by De Morgan's theorem allows the *equal* sign to remain.

Because the negate operation changes the valuation of a function from 1 to 0 or from 0 to 1, it is usually called the *complement* function.

EXAMPLE 2.5

Using the basic theorems, find the complement of

$$F = (X + Y) \cdot \left(\overline{XY} + \overline{X}\,\overline{Y} \right)$$

The complement can be obtained by applying De Morgan's theorem. The best approach is to treat each parenthetical term as a single variable. The process starts by complementing *both* sides of the equation.

$$\overline{F} = \overline{(X + Y) \cdot \left(\overline{XY} + \overline{X}\,\overline{Y} \right)}$$

$$= \overline{(X + Y)} + \overline{\left(\overline{XY} + \overline{X}\,\overline{Y} \right)}$$

De Morgan's theorem can now be successively applied, beginning with the largest groups:

$$\overline{F} = \overline{X}\,\overline{Y} + \left(\overline{\overline{XY}} \cdot \overline{\overline{X}\,\overline{Y}} \right)$$

$$= \overline{X}\,\overline{Y} + (XY \cdot [X + Y])$$

$$= \overline{X}\,\overline{Y} + (XYX + XYY)$$

$$= \overline{X}\,\overline{Y} + XY + XY$$

$$\overline{F} = \overline{X}\,\overline{Y} + XY$$

The Expansion Theorem

Theorem 11 is a technique for expanding a function which is in a simplified form about each of its variables. The resultant expression contains *all* the unreduced terms of the function. It is a means of placing an expression into a standard form.

EXAMPLE 2.6

Using the expansion theorem, prove that the function $F = X + Y$ is identical to another function $G = X + \overline{X}Y$.

1. Apply the expansion theorem to the function

   $$F = X + Y$$

   First, expanding about X by using the expression

   $$F/_x(X, Y) = XF(1, Y) + \overline{X}F(0, Y)$$

   $$F/_x = X(1 + Y) + \overline{X}(0 + Y)$$

   $$= X + XY + \overline{X}Y$$

   Now expanding the resultant expression $(F/_x)$ about y using the expression

   $$F/_x/_y(X, Y) = YF/_x(X, 1) + \overline{Y}F/_x(X, 0)$$

   $$F/_x/_y = Y(X + X + \overline{X}) + \overline{Y}(X + 0 + 0)$$

   $$= XY + XY + Y\overline{X} + \overline{Y}X$$

   $$F/_x/_y = XY + \overline{X}Y + X\overline{Y}$$

   Note that the resulting function of X and Y contains three product terms, in which *all* the variables, X and Y, are contained in each term.

2. If we now take the other function

   $$G = X + \overline{X}Y$$

   First, expanding about X:

   $$G/_x = X(1 + 0) + \overline{X}(0 + Y)$$

   $$= X + \overline{X}Y$$

   Now expanding about Y:

   $$G/_x/_y = Y(X + \overline{X}) + \overline{Y}(X + 0)$$

   $$G/_x/_y = XY + \overline{X}Y + X\overline{Y}$$

   (thus proving the equality of F and G).

EXAMPLE 2.7

Given the function $F = \bar{X} + \bar{Y} + YZ$, expand F about X, Y, and Z.

$$F = \bar{X} + \bar{Y} + YZ$$

$$F/_x = X(\bar{Y} + YZ) + \bar{X}(1 + \bar{Y} + YZ)$$

$$= X\bar{Y} + XYZ + \bar{X} + \bar{X}\bar{Y} + \bar{X}YZ$$

$$F/_x/_y = Y(XZ + \bar{X} + \bar{X}Z) + \bar{Y}(X + \bar{X} + \bar{X})$$

$$= XYZ + \bar{X}Y + \bar{X}YZ + X\bar{Y} + \bar{X}\bar{Y}$$

$$F/_x/_y/_z = Z(XY + \bar{X}Y + \bar{X}Y + X\bar{Y} + \bar{X}\bar{Y}) + \bar{Z}(\bar{X}Y + X\bar{Y} + \bar{X}\bar{Y})$$

$$= XYZ + \bar{X}YZ + X\bar{Y}Z + \bar{X}\bar{Y}Z + \bar{X}Y\bar{Z} + X\bar{Y}\bar{Z} + \bar{X}\bar{Y}\bar{Z}$$

2.3 DESCRIPTORS

There are a variety of models that can be used to describe Boolean functions, some more useful than others. As an aid to understanding Boolean functions, we will examine some of these models, which are herein more appropriately labeled as *descriptors*.

Specifically, we will look at

1. Truth tables and Karnaugh maps
2. The classical Venn diagram
3. Switching circuits
4. Logic circuits

The logic circuit model has the most significance for this discussion, since this is the technique for implementing Boolean equations in a digital computer.

To have a common reference for all descriptors, it is important to develop a standard form for all Boolean functions. Consider a universal set that contains the elements A and B, both of which are Boolean variables. The universal set can be itself described as a Boolean function $S(\cup)$ that consists of *all* the combinations of A and B. By using the truth calculus interpretation, all the combinations of the set are described in table 2-2.

Table 2-2   Combinations of the Universal Set for Two Variables

A	B	$S(\cup)$
F	F	NOT A and NOT B
F	T	NOT A AND B
T	F	A AND NOT B
T	T	A AND B

By extracting all the combinations, the universal set can be written in a single sentence in semiequation form:

$$S(\cup) = (\text{NOT } A \text{ and NOT } B) \text{ OR } (\text{NOT } A \text{ AND } B) \qquad \text{(Eq. 2-1)}$$

$$\text{OR } (A \text{ AND NOT } B) \text{ OR } (A \text{ AND } B)$$

Table 2-2 can be further expanded to describe the universal set using the notation of the set theory and Boolean algebra interpretations, as table 2-3 shows.

From table 2-3 we see that for the universal set to be 1 (or true), each of the four product terms must also be 1. It should be evident from this that *all* functions of two variables are a *subset* of the universal set. That is, each subset will consist of some combination of terms which are contained in the universal set.

Thus, if each product term in the table is multiplied by a binary constant a_i, which is either 1 or 0, then we have a means of describing all possible combinations of two variables.

It is convenient to standardize on the means of *labeling* each a_i term. For each *binary* combination of A and B, there is a constant a_i in which the i subscript is assigned a *decimal* equivalent obtained directly from the valuation of the variables in each term. That is, for the $A\overline{B}$ term to be true, $A = 1$ and $B = 0$ must hold. Therefore, the $A\overline{B}$ term can be described by a base 2 number $(10)_2$, which in turn has a decimal equivalent $(2)_{10}$. Thus for $a_i A\overline{B}$, $a_i = a_2$ and we have the term $a_2 A\overline{B}$.

Table 2-3   Combinations of the Universal Set $S(\cup)$

A	B	Truth Calculus	Set Theory	Boolean Algebra	
0	0	$\sim A \wedge \sim B$	$\overline{A} \cap \overline{B}$	$\overline{A}$	$\overline{B}$
0	1	$\sim A \wedge B$	$\overline{A} \cap B$	$\overline{A}$	B
1	0	$A \wedge \sim B$	$A \cap \overline{B}$	A	$\overline{B}$
1	1	$A \wedge B$	$A \cap B$	A	B

We can proceed to generate a *general form* for a two-variable Boolean function, using Boolean variables to describe all the possible combinations of equation 2-1.

$$f(A,B) = a_0 \overline{A}\,\overline{B} + a_1 \overline{A}\,B + a_2 A\overline{B} + a_3 AB = \sum_{i=0}^{3} a_i P_i \qquad \text{(Eq. 2-2)}$$

where P_i represents each product term.

EXAMPLE 2.8

Show the Boolean function of two variables for which the $i=2$ and $i=3$ product terms are 1.

For $a_2 = a_3 = 1$ and $a_0 = a_1 = 0$, the standard form reduces to

$$F_{2,3} = 0 \cdot \overline{A}\,\overline{B} + 0 \cdot \overline{A}\,B + 1 \cdot A\overline{B} + 1 \cdot AB$$

$$= A\overline{B} + AB = A(\overline{B} + B)$$

$$= A$$

Truth Tables and Karnaugh Maps

Examination of the general form for two variables

$$f(A,B) = a_0 \overline{A}\,\overline{B} + a_1 \overline{A}\,B + a_2 A\overline{B} + a_3 AB \qquad \text{(Eq. 2-2)}$$

indicates that a very specific number of functions of two variables are possible. Depending on whether each a_i is 1 or 0, there are $2 \cdot 2 \cdot 2 \cdot 2 = 2^4 = 16$ possible functions. Each of these functions can be shown in a tabular manner by a truth table; it shows which terms are true (1) and which are false (0). Table 2-4 is a truth table for the functions $F_{0,3}$ and $F_{0,1,3}$.

Table 2-4   Truth Table

A	B	Combinations of AB	a_i	$F_{0,3} = \overline{A}\,\overline{B} + AB$	$F_{0,1,3} = \overline{A} + AB$
0	0	$\overline{A}\,\overline{B}$	a_0	1	1
0	1	$\overline{A}\,B$	a_1	0	1
1	0	$A\overline{B}$	a_2	0	0
1	1	AB	a_3	1	1

Quite often, the rationale of a logic function becomes apparent by examining both the truth table and the methodology of the truth calculus. In the case of $F_{0,1,3} = \overline{A} + AB$, the $\overline{A}$ term means that the function is true whenever $\overline{A}$ is true. In the truth table, $\overline{A}$ is true for both the $a_0 \overline{A}\,\overline{B}$ and the $a_1 \overline{A} B$ terms, regardless of the valuation of B. Thus a_0 and a_1 are both 1 in the truth table. The function is also true whenever the AB term is true. Because this term is unique, $a_3 = 1$ completes the description of the function $F_{0,1,3}$.

EXAMPLE 2.9

For a function of three variables $f(A,B,C)$, the output is true whenever *two or more* variables are true. Show the truth table for the function.

By setting up a table that lists all the combinations, each term can be examined to see if it satisfies the criterion for this function. Terms in the form $AB\overline{C}, A\overline{B}C, \overline{A}BC, \ldots$, have two noncomplemented terms, so they would equal 1. Also the term ABC has *at least* two 1's, so it would also be true. Table 2-5 shows the completed truth table.

Although the truth table gives a complete description, the relationship between a simplified and an expanded function as shown in table 2-5 lacks an ease of utilization. In particular, one of the main concerns with manipulating logic functions is to be able to minimize an expanded function to as few terms as possible. Because all logic functions eventually convert to logic circuits in a computer, any reductions obtained will become apparent in the reduced amount of computer circuits.

The most effective minimization technique is a variation of the truth table called the *Karnaugh map* (figure 2-3). The two-variable Karnaugh map is simply a grid of all truth table combinations. The basic concept behind the map is to reduce functions such as $AB + A\overline{B} = A(B + \overline{B}) = A$ by utilizing the relationship $(B + \overline{B}) = 1$.

Table 2-5   Completed Truth Table

A	B	C	Combinations of A,B,C	$f(A,B,C)$
0	0	0	$\overline{A}\,\overline{B}\,\overline{C}$	0
0	0	1	$\overline{A}\,\overline{B}C$	0
0	1	0	$\overline{A}B\overline{C}$	0
0	1	1	$\overline{A}BC$	1
1	0	0	$A\overline{B}\,\overline{C}$	0
1	0	1	$A\overline{B}C$	1
1	1	0	$AB\overline{C}$	1
1	1	1	ABC	1

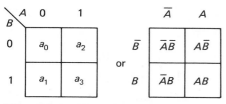

Figure 2-3   The Karnaugh Map

If all variables can be gridded so that ones and zeros (or B and $\bar{B}$) are on adjacent squares, then B and $\bar{B}$ can be eliminated from the expression by looking for adjacent squares on the map.

EXAMPLE 2.10

Reduce the function $F_{0,1,3} = \overline{A}\overline{B} + \overline{A}B + AB$. $F_{0,1,3}$ has the map shown in figure 2-4.

The adjacency of B and $\bar{B}$ in the a_0 and a_1 squares results in $\overline{A}\overline{B} + \overline{A}B = \overline{A}(\overline{B}+B) = \overline{A}$. This is shown in figure 2-5.

Thus it is seen that the function can be reduced to

$$F_{0,1,3} = \overline{A}\,\overline{B} + \overline{A}\,B + AB$$

$$= \overline{A}(\overline{B}+B) + AB = \overline{A} + AB$$

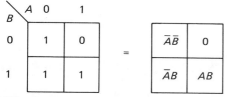

Figure 2-4

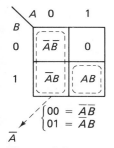

Figure 2-5

Further reduction can be obtained by using adjacencies to eliminate superfluous terms. This is shown in figure 2-6, where the $a_1\overline{A}B$ term is shared by *both* groups.

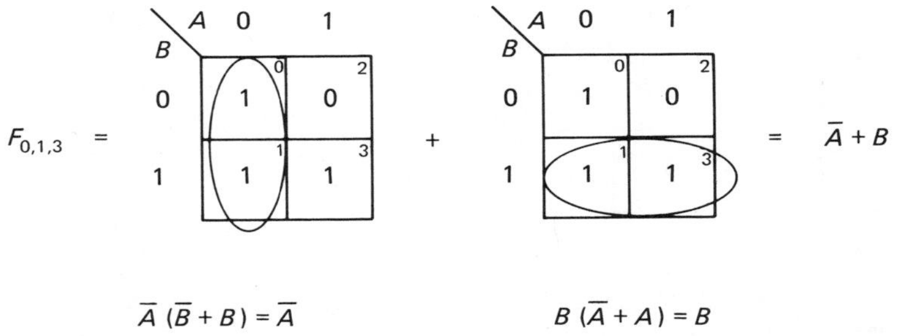

$F_{0,1,3}$ = [map] + [map] = $\overline{A} + B$

$\overline{A}(\overline{B} + B) = \overline{A}$ $B(\overline{A} + A) = B$

Figure 2-6

By using the map, the adjacencies can be obtained with relative simplicity.

To perform the same reduction algebraically, the following would be done:

$$F_{0,1,3} = \overline{A}\,\overline{B} + \overline{A}\,B + AB$$

$$= (\underbrace{\overline{A}\,\overline{B}}_{a_0} + \underbrace{\overline{A}\,B}_{a_1}) + (\underbrace{\overline{A}\,B}_{a_1} + \underbrace{AB}_{a_3})$$

$$= \overline{A}(\overline{B} + B) + B(\overline{A} + A)$$

$$= \overline{A} + B$$

EXAMPLE 2.11

Using the Karnaugh map, simplify $F_{1,2,3} = \overline{A}B + A\overline{B} + AB$. The map in figure 2-7 shows the function.

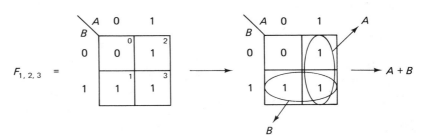

$F_{1,2,3}$ =

Figure 2-7

For two variables, all the possible adjacencies are shown in figure 2-8.

In a later section on minimization, functions of greater than two variables will be examined.

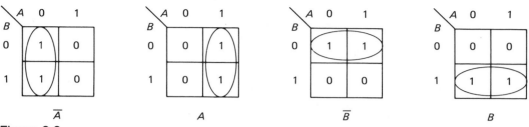

Figure 2-8

The Venn Diagram

The Venn diagram is a diagrammatic descriptor of Boolean algebra that relates particularly well to the set theory interpretation. It is named after John Venn, who presented the technique in 1880.

Figure 2-9 shows the Venn model, which contains the elements (A, B) as two overlapping circles. All portions of the rectangle, in and out of the circles, represent the universal set. The *null set*, which is the complement of the universal set, has no area.

Using the general form for the Boolean function of two variables,

$$f(A, B) = a_0 \overline{A}\,\overline{B} + a_1 \overline{A}\,B + a_2 A\overline{B} + a_3 AB \qquad \text{(Eq. 2-2)}$$

each term can be appropriately located on the Venn diagram (figure 2-10).

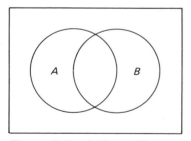

Figure 2-9   A Venn Diagram

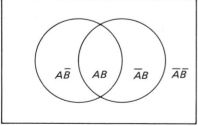

Figure 2-10   Locating Terms in a Venn Diagram

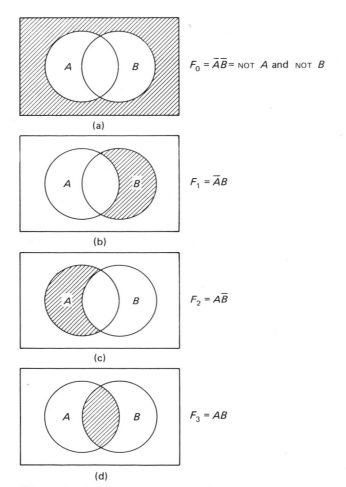

(a)

(b)

(c)

(d)

Figure 2-11

The diagram can now be examined for each case in which only one of the product terms is true (figure 2-11).

By superimposing all four diagrams, the result is the universal set (figure 2-12).

The Venn diagram will also describe combinations of functions, such as figure 2-13.

From the diagram for the function G, it becomes quite evident that

$$G = \overline{A}B + AB = B$$

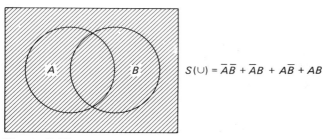

$S(\cup) = \bar{A}\bar{B} + \bar{A}B + A\bar{B} + AB$

Figure 2-12

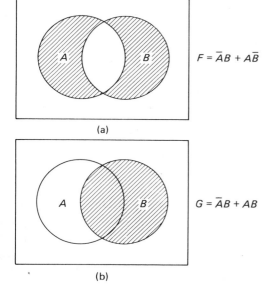

$F = \bar{A}B + A\bar{B}$

(a)

$G = \bar{A}B + AB$

(b)

Figure 2-13

which we can also see algebraically:

$$G = \bar{A}B + AB = B(\bar{A} + A)$$
$$= B$$

The Venn diagram serves in this manner to show pictorially *all* the component terms of a Boolean function.

EXAMPLE 2.12

Using the Venn diagram, obtain all the product terms for $F = A + B$. By using figure 2-14, this becomes a trivial exercise in which

$$F = A + B = A\bar{B} + AB + \bar{A}B$$

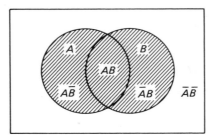

Figure 2-14

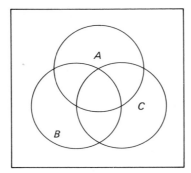

Figure 2-15

The Venn diagram can also be used for more than two variables (see figure 2-15), although extending beyond three becomes rather difficult.

If we take any function of three variables, such as $F = A\bar{B}C + A\bar{B}\bar{C}$, with a bit of care, we can place it on a three-variable diagram (figure 2-16). From the diagram, it can be determined that this function reduces to $F = A\bar{B}$.

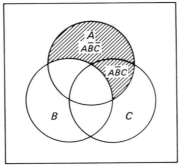

Figure 2-16

Figure 2-17 shows all the components of a three-variable universal set.

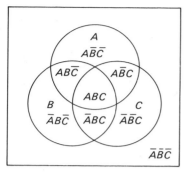

Figure 2-17

Switching Circuits

The interpretation of the logic of Boolean algebra is nicely demonstrated by the use of switching circuits as a descriptor. This is conveniently shown by using the switching relay as a basic logic element (figure 2-18).

The symbol in figure 2-18 denotes a relay (or switch) contact X which is normally open. During the period of operation, which is the period when a Boolean equation describes the circuit, the relay will switch closed if X operates. For this condition $X = 1$ or true. This will generate a path for current from point 1 to point 2, the path thus becoming a short circuit.

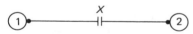

Figure 2-18

If $X = 0$ or false, then the relay does not operate (it remains open) and the path for current remains an open circuit. The logical operation of this relay is completely described in table 2-6.

Table 2-6   Normally Open Relay

Relay	Path	X
Operate	Short	1
Not Operate	Open	0

Conversely, there are also normally closed relays (figure 2-19) which are a short circuit path from point 1 to 2 when X does NOT open during the period of operation. That is, the path remains closed as long as the condition of $X = 0$ or false is retained. Thus this relay is labeled $\overline{X}$. Whenever $X = 1$ does occur, the relay operates by *opening*, and the current

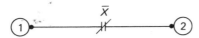

Figure 2-19

path from point 1 to 2 is described as $\overline{X}=0$. The logical operation of the normally closed relay is completely described in table 2-7.

Table 2-7   Normally Closed Relay

Relay	Path	$\overline{X}$	X
Operate	Open	0	1
Not operate	Short	1	0

The fascination of using switching circuit networks as a descriptor is that the requirement for transmission between two points is a very diagrammatic method for showing a logic function, as the following examples show.

EXAMPLE 2.13

1. Show the logic equation for the relay circuit in figure 2-20. The path from 1 to 2 requires either Z OR Y to close (or operate), AND NO operation of X. This can be described as:

$$F=\overline{X}(Y+Z)$$

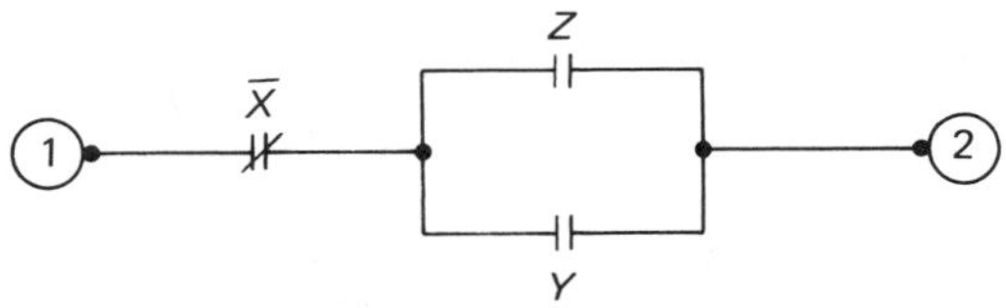

Figure 2-20

2. Show the logic equation for the circuit in figure 2-21. In this case, transmission requires either X OR Y to close, AND also Z OR NOT W. The equation is:

$$F=(X+Y)(Z+\overline{W})$$

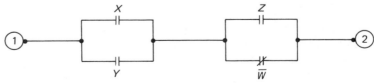

Figure 2-21

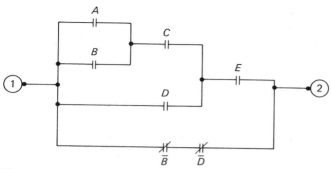

Figure 2-22

3. Write the logic equation which describes the relay circuit in figure 2-22. Tracing the topology from point 1 to 2 the following equation results (figure 2-22):

$$F = [(A+B)C+D]E + \overline{B}\,\overline{D}$$

EXAMPLE 2.14

Show the equation and the relay network for the transmission that is required for the following statement:

Transmission occurs if Y OR Z close whenever (AND) X closes, OR alternately when W does NOT open. The network is shown in figure 2-23. From the diagram the equation is obtained:

$$F = X(Y+Z) + \overline{W}$$

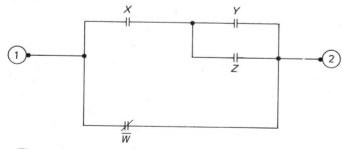

Figure 2-23

The general Boolean form for two variables

$$f(A,B) = a_0\overline{A}\,\overline{B} + a_1\overline{A}B + a_2A\overline{B} + a_3AB$$

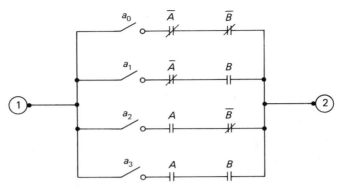

Figure 2-24

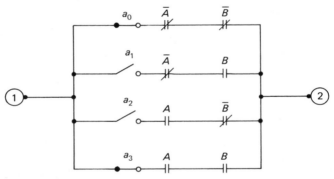

Figure 2-25

is shown as a generalized relay network in figure 2-24. The closing of the appropriate a_i switches will result in any of the possible functions which can be formed by two variables. Thus a function such as $F = \overline{A}\overline{B} + AB$ can be described as in figure 2-25.

Logic Circuits

Electronic circuits formed by transistors and diodes are used in computers to perform the equivalent of the logic operations described by Boolean equations. These are the fundamental elements of a computer structure. There is a basic analogy between using bricks to implement the architectural plan of a building and the use of logic circuits (or gates) as the building blocks to implement a computer architecture.

As a means of conveniently describing logic circuits, logic symbols are used which are a descriptor of a Boolean expression, as in figure 2-26.

These logic symbols represent some type of electronic circuit that is performing the logic function. Different electronic components, such as

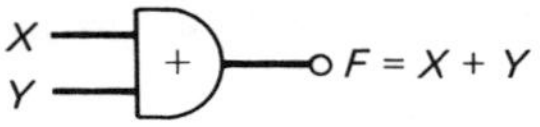

Figure 2-26

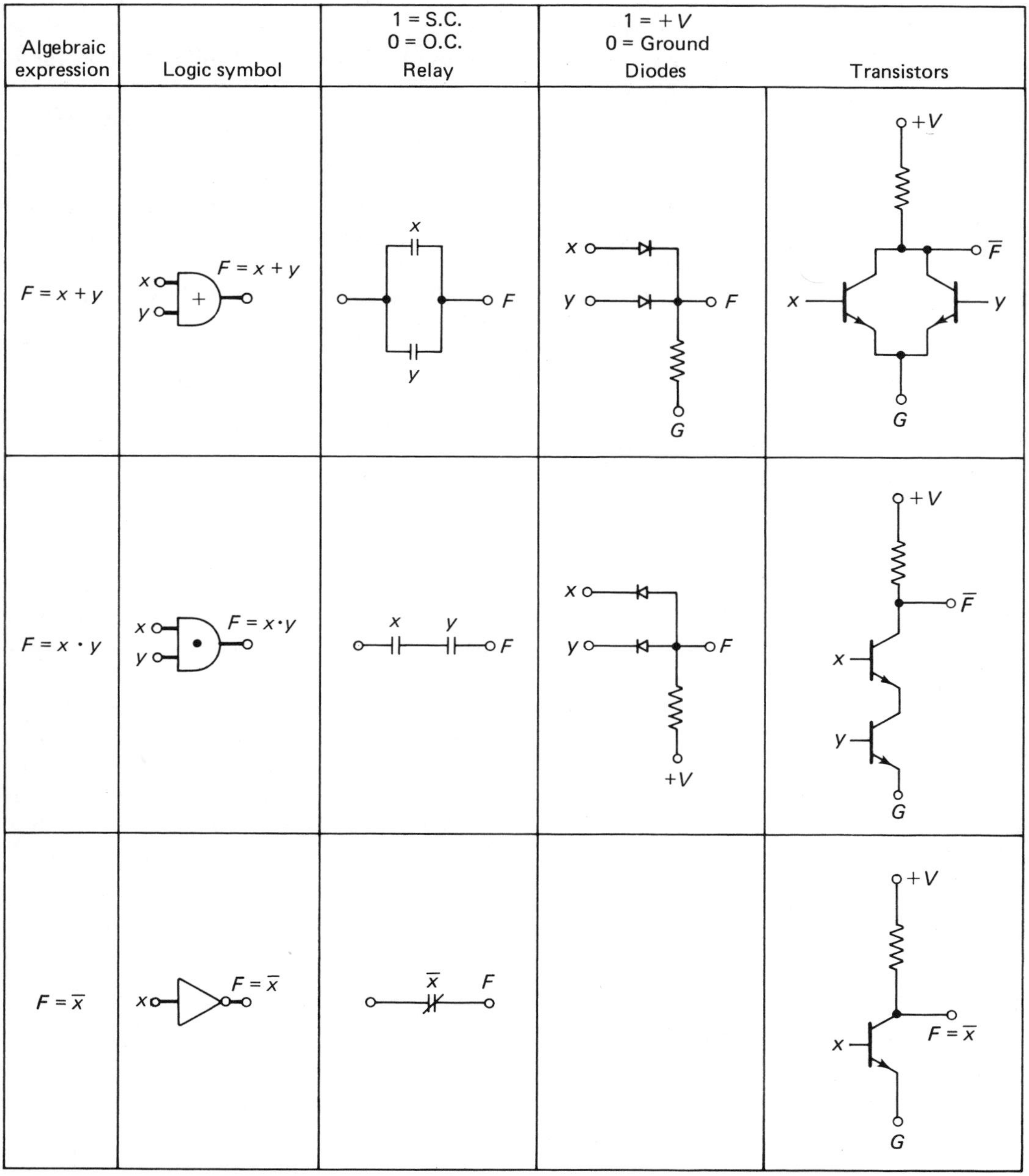

Figure 2-27 Basic Logic Circuits

transistors or diodes, will actually have various configurations that perform the same specific logic function. Thus the logic symbol is independent of the particular electronic circuit which is actually used. In figure 2-27, the logic symbol is shown for each basic Boolean operation, together with some representative electronic circuits. For comparison, the equivalent relay switching circuit is also shown. In this section we will show how these electronic circuits are formed.

An examination of electronic circuits will show that the primary logic difference from relay switches is in the method of representing the 1 or 0 valuation of a variable. Relays represent a 1 by establishing a path for electric current, and a lack of path is represented by 0. In electronic circuits a voltage level at the device represents the 1 or 0 valuation.

For example, in a relay the normally closed circuit defines the NOT logic function, because current always passes ($F=1$) if we have NOT X (X not operated), as in figure 2-28.

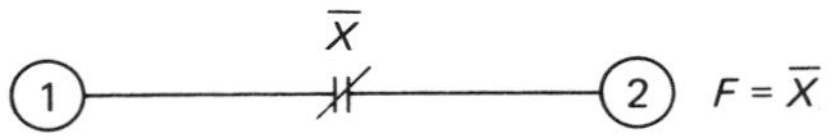

①————————$\overline{X}$⊬————————② $F = \overline{X}$

Figure 2-28 NOT X

X ○————————▷○————————○ $F = \overline{X}$

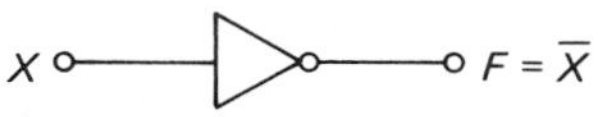

Figure 2-29 NOT X

However, in an electronic circuit the NOT function will occur when the output voltage is at the opposite *level* (or complement) of the input level, as in figure 2-29.

This can be clarified by examining a transistor inverter, as in figure 2-30. The transistor is considered here for the simplified case in which only two voltage levels are allowed. That is, the INPUT and OUTPUT can be either $+V$ or G. $+V$ is a positive voltage, between 5 and 12 volts, depending on the type of circuit. This will represent a logic 1. G is ground level, which is zero volts. This will be a logic 0.

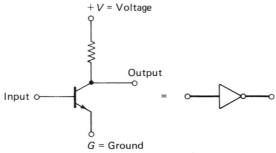

Figure 2-30   A Transistor Inverter

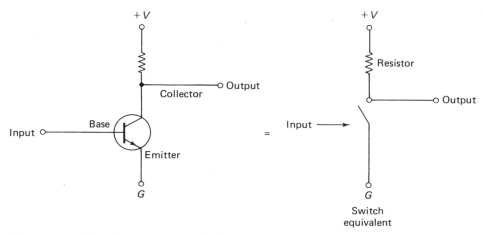

Figure 2-31 The Transistor as a Switch

The transistor shown in figure 2-30 has three ports, or points of access, each of which has its own name, as shown in figure 2-31. The input is applied to the *base* and the output is at the *collector*. In this configuration, the device can be simply represented as a switch which is controlled inside the transistor by the voltage at the base. A positive voltage ($+V$) at the base "closes the switch," allowing full conduction from collector to emitter, so that the transistor is turned on and the emitter voltage level (G) is presented to the output. The resistor in the circuit is necessary as a load, so that the $+V$ power source is isolated from the 0 volts at ground.

An input of zero at the base "opens the switch" and does not allow collector to emitter conduction, so that the transistor is turned off. Thus the $+V$ voltage appears at the output.

The next two cases examine the transistor performing the logic inversion operation:

CASE 1

$$\boxed{\text{IN} = \text{LOGIC } 1 = +V}$$

When a positive voltage is applied at the input, the transistor is turned on, so that the equivalent circuit is shown in figure 2-32.

CASE 2

$$\boxed{\text{IN} = \text{LOGIC } 0 = G}$$

When ground, or 0 volts, is applied at the input, the transistor is turned off, so that the equivalent circuit is shown in figure 2-33. Therefore, the truth

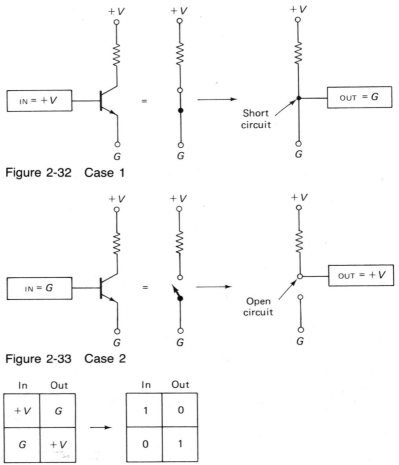

Figure 2-32   Case 1

Figure 2-33   Case 2

In	Out
+V	G
G	+V

In	Out
1	0
0	1

Figure 2-34   Transistor Inverter Truth Table

table in figure 2-34 will hold. Thus, the circuit configuration in figure 2-35 is shown with its equivalent logic symbol.

The AND and OR logic circuits can be described by using a device called a *diode*. The main characteristic of the diode is that it conducts current in only one direction—that is, from higher voltage ($+V$) to lower voltage ($G=0V$), in the direction of the arrow ($\rightarrow$), as shown in figure 2-36.

These characteristics are used to form logic gates which perform the desired function, such as the OR gate in figure 2-37. For this gate, a $+V$ will appear at the output when either X OR Y or both are at $+V$.

For an AND gate, there is also a diode configuration which will perform the appropriate logic function, as in figure 2-38. Note that any

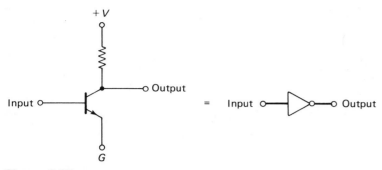

Figure 2-35

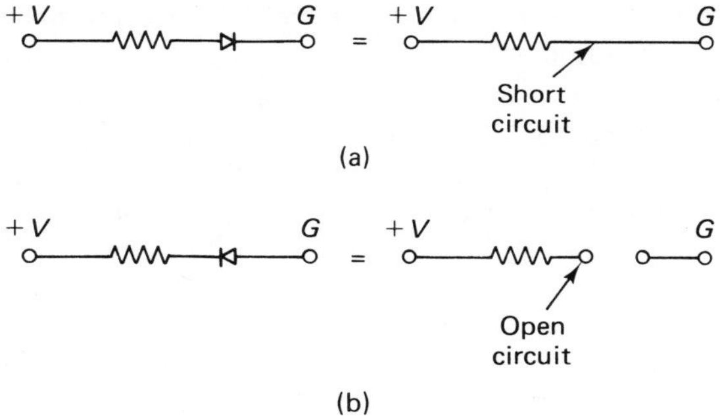

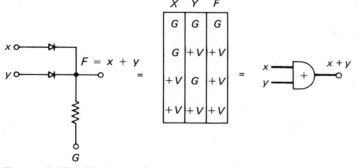

Figure 2-36   Diode Characteristics

$$F = x + y$$

X	Y	F
G	G	G
G	+V	+V
+V	G	+V
+V	+V	+V

Figure 2-37   Diode OR Gate

$F = x \cdot y$

X	Y	F
G	G	G
G	+V	G
+V	G	G
+V	+V	+V

$x \cdot y$

Figure 2-38   Diode AND Gate

time an input is at ground, the diode will conduct, thus allowing a ground at the output. When both inputs are at $+V$, then $+V$ is at the output and the conditions for an AND gate are satisfied.

Logic gates may also be made up from transistor inverters by forming appropriate configurations, such as that in figure 2-39. In this case, if either X OR Y are at $+V$, that transistor will conduct and place a ground at F. Thus the output function is NOT OR or NOR as shown in figure 2-40.

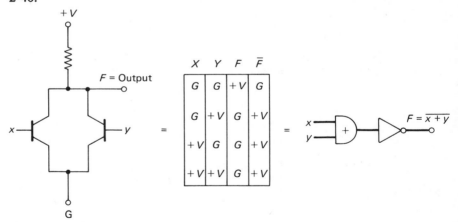

$+V$

$F = $ Output

X	Y	F	$\bar{F}$
G	G	+V	G
G	+V	G	+V
+V	G	G	+V
+V	+V	G	+V

$F = \overline{x + y}$

G

Figure 2-39   NOR Gate

The OR function can be derived from the NOR by placing an inverter at the output of the NOR as in figure 2-41.

A slightly different configuration can be used to derive an AND function (figure 2-42). In this circuit both X and Y have to place a positive voltage at the transistor bases in order to have conduction from ground to F. This results in the NOT AND or NAND logic function of figure 2-43. This can be used to form an AND function by adding an inverter in the same manner as was done for the NOR. This is shown in figure 2-44.

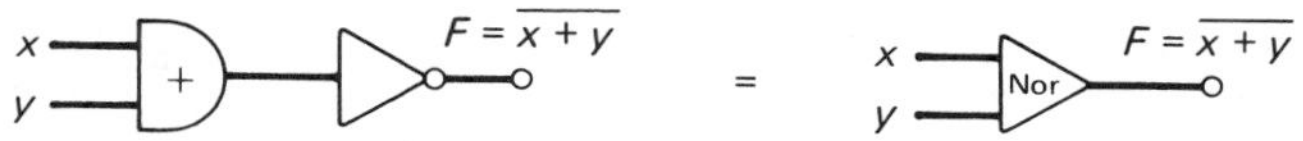

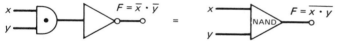

Figure 2-40 Equivalent NOR Gate

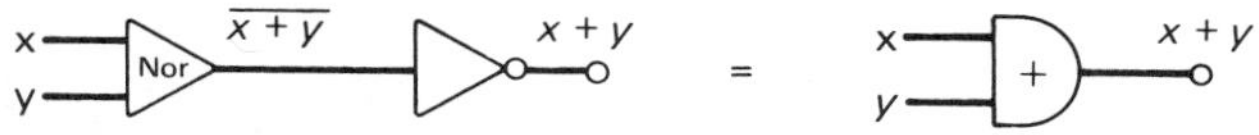

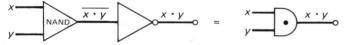

Figure 2-41 Equivalent OR Gate

=

X	Y	F	$\overline{F}$
G	G	+V	G
G	+V	+V	G
+V	G	+V	G
+V	+V	+G	+V

=

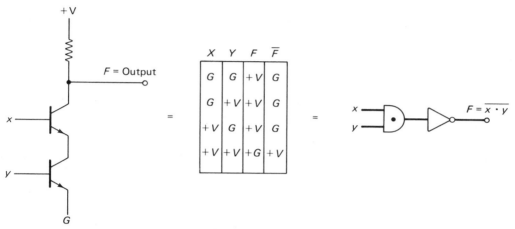

Figure 2-42 NAND Gate

Figure 2-43 Equivalent NAND Gate

Figure 2-44 Equivalent AND Gate

EXAMPLE 2.15

Using logic circuits (AND, OR, and NOT), diagram the function $F=\overline{(AB\overline{C}+\overline{DEF})}\,\overline{(\overline{D}E)}+\overline{Q}$.

If care is taken to use an inverter for any function which is complemented, the logic in figure 2-45 results.

The earlier switching circuit example of $F=X\cdot(Y+Z)+\overline{W}$ can be described with logic symbols, as in figure 2-46. In this manner it is quite

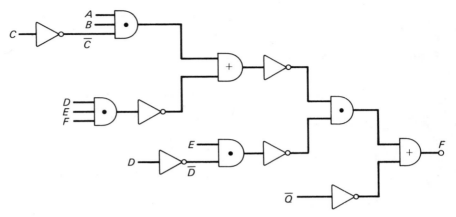

Figure 2-45

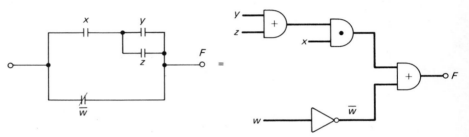

Figure 2-46   Logic Equivalent to Relay Circuit

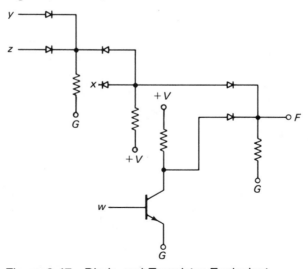

Figure 2-47   Diode and Transistor Equivalent

simple to implement F with *any* set of logic devices. For example, by using diodes and transistors (with levels as defined in figure 2-27), the circuit of figure 2-47 defines $F = X \cdot (Y + Z) + \overline{W}$.

2.4 CANONICAL FORMS

A canonical (or standard) form of a Boolean function is an expanded description which uniquely gives all the combinations of the functions.

The standard sum form (equation 2-2) is one canonical form, in which functions are described by the summation of product terms. Each of these product terms includes all the variables that compose the functions. For example, using

$$f(A, B) = a_0 \overline{A}\,\overline{B} + a_1 A \overline{B} + a_2 \overline{A} B + a_3 A B \qquad \text{(Eq. 2-2)}$$

as the standard sum canonical form will uniquely describe all functions of two variables. This description is of course determined by the valuation of a_i. The use of the expansion theorem

$$F(X, Y, Z) = X \cdot F(1, Y, Z) + \overline{X} \cdot F(0, Y, Z)$$

is a systematic technique for generating the canonical form by expanding about each variable.

For example, take the function

$$f = X + Y + Z$$

If we first expand about X:

$$F/_X = X(1 + Y + Z) + \overline{X}(0 + Y + Z)$$

$$= X + XY + XZ + \overline{X}Y + \overline{X}Z$$

We next expand the resulting function about Y:

$$F_X/_Y = Y(X + X \cdot 1 + XZ + \overline{X} \cdot 1 + \overline{X}Z)$$

$$+ \overline{Y}(X + XZ + \overline{X}Z)$$

$$= XY + XYZ + \overline{X}\,Y + \overline{X}\,YZ + X\overline{Y} + X\overline{Y}Z + \overline{X}\,\overline{Y}Z$$

Next we expand about Z:

$$F_{X,Y}/_Z = Z(XY + \bar{X}Y + X\bar{Y} + \bar{X}\bar{Y}) + \bar{Z}(XY + \bar{X}Y + X\bar{Y})$$

$$= \underset{7}{XYZ} + \underset{3}{\bar{X}YZ} + \underset{5}{X\bar{Y}Z} + \underset{1}{\bar{X}\bar{Y}Z} + \underset{6}{XY\bar{Z}} + \underset{2}{\bar{X}Y\bar{Z}} + \underset{4}{X\bar{Y}\bar{Z}}$$

The result gives the a_i terms for $i = 1,2,3,4,5,6,7$. This follows, because to have $X + Y + Z$, every term is required except $\bar{X}\bar{Y}\bar{Z}$, which is a_0.

This brings us to the desirability of using a shorthand notation to express the a_i terms in the standard sum. Instead of the expression $f = \sum_{i=0}^{2^n} a_i P_i$, where P_i is each canonical product term, it is more convenient to write the expression as follows:

$$f = X + Y + Z = \sum (1,2,3,4,5,6,7)$$

in which each of the i subscripts of the standard form are listed.

The Standard Product

Another standard form is the *product of sums*. The standard form for this can be evolved from the equation of the standard sum,

$$F(A,B) = a_0\bar{A}\bar{B} + a_1\bar{A}B + a_2A\bar{B} + a_3AB \qquad \text{(Eq. 2-2)}$$

$$= \sum_{i=0}^{3} a_i P_i$$

By applying De Morgan's theorem, we first obtain a standard product of *sums* for the complemented function $\overline{F(A,B)}$.

$$\overline{F(A,B)} = \overline{a_0\bar{A}\bar{B} + a_1\bar{A}B + a_2A\bar{B} + a_3AB}$$

$$= \left(\bar{a}_0 + \overline{\bar{A}\bar{B}}\right)\left(\bar{a}_1 + \overline{\bar{A}B}\right)\left(\bar{a}_2 + \overline{A\bar{B}}\right)\left(\bar{a}_3 + \overline{AB}\right)$$

so that

$$\overline{F(A,B)} = \left(\bar{a}_0 + A + B\right)\left(\bar{a}_1 + A + \bar{B}\right)\left(\bar{a}_2 + \bar{A} + B\right)\left(\bar{a}_3 + \bar{A} + \bar{B}\right)$$

$$\text{(Eq. 2-3a)}$$

By using $\prod$ as the symbol for "the product of," the standard form for $\overline{F(A,B)}$ can be expressed as

$$\overline{F(A,B)} = \prod_{i=0}^{3} (\bar{a}_i + S_i) \qquad \text{(Eq. 2-3b)}$$

Note that each sum term (which is commonly labeled as an S term) is the complement of the corresponding P term. That is

$$P_i = \overline{S_i}$$

Thus, for a term with two variables and an $i=2$,

for $P_2 = A\bar{B}$ and $S_2 = \bar{A} + B$

it is evident that $A\bar{B} = \overline{\bar{A} + B}$

By using a similar approach, a standard product of *sums* can also be obtained for the uncomplemented $F(A,B)$.

First, we must express $\overline{F(A,B)}$ in a standard sum of *products* form. Since

$$F(A,B) + \overline{F(A,B)} = 1$$

must be true, as they contain all elements of the universal set, then it is evident that if

$$F(A,B) = \sum_{i=0}^{2^n} a_i P_i$$

then

$$\overline{F(A,B)} = \sum_{i=0}^{2^n} \bar{a}_i P_i$$

so that $F(A,B)$ can be expressed as a function of $\bar{a}_i$:

$$F(A,B) = \overline{\sum_{i=0}^{2^n} \bar{a}_i P_i}$$

By applying De Morgan's theorem to the latter we can obtain the standard product of *sums* for $F(A,B)$ as follows:

$$F(A,B) = \overline{\bar{a}_0\bar{A}\,\bar{B} + \bar{a}_1\bar{A}\,B + \bar{a}_2A\bar{B} + \bar{a}_3AB}$$

and

$$F(A,B) = (a_0 + A + B)(a_1 + A + \bar{B})(a_2 + \bar{A} + B)(a_3 + \bar{A} + \bar{B})$$

(Eq. 2-4a)

$$F(A,B) = \prod_{i=0}^{3} (a_i + S_i)$$

(Eq. 2-4b)

Various standard forms are summarized in table 2-8.

Table 2-8

	Sum of *Products*	Products of *Sums*
$F(A,B)$	$F = \sum_{i=0}^{3} a_i P_i$	$F = \prod_{i=0}^{3} (a_i + S_i)$
$\overline{F(A,B)}$	$\bar{F} = \sum_{i=0}^{3} \bar{a}_i P_i$	$\bar{F} = \prod_{i=0}^{3} (\bar{a}_i + S_i)$

To make the functions less painful to form, it is helpful to establish a table for the a_i's and their corresponding P and S terms as in table 2-9.

Table 2-9

a_i	P_i	S_i
a_0	$\bar{A}\bar{B}$	$A + B$
a_1	$\bar{A}B$	$A + \bar{B}$
a_2	$A\bar{B}$	$\bar{A} + B$
a_3	AB	$\bar{A} + \bar{B}$

Example 2.16 shows the use of the standard form in describing a specific function.

EXAMPLE 2.16

The function $F = \Sigma(1,2)$ is often called the "exclusive or" operator. The Boolean OR is an "inclusive or" in which its operation is on A or B or *both*, whereas the "exclusive or" is an operation on A or B but *not* both.

Express this function and its complement in both sum of *products* and product of *sums* form.

From the format of the function $F = \Sigma(1,2)$,

$$a_1 = a_2 = 1, \quad \text{and} \quad a_0 + a_3 = 0$$

Thus from table 2-9, in the sum of *products* form:

$$F = \sum_{i=0}^{3} a_i P_i = \underbrace{\overline{A}B}_{i=1} + \underbrace{A\overline{B}}_{i=2}$$

and

$$\overline{F} = \sum_{i=0}^{3} \overline{a}_i P_i = \underbrace{\overline{A}\,\overline{B}}_{i=0} + \underbrace{AB}_{i=3}$$

For the product of *sums* form, note that when $a_i = 1$, the S_i term will disappear because of the $(1 + S_i)$ operation, and that *only* the a_0 and a_3 terms remain.

$$F = \prod_{i=0}^{3} (a_i + S_i) = \left(\overset{0}{\overset{/\!/}{a_0}} + A + B \right)\left(\overset{0}{\overset{/\!/}{a_3}} + \overline{A} + \overline{B} \right)$$

$$= (A + B)(\overline{A} + \overline{B})$$

since $a_0 = a_3 = 0$

Also, for the complement,

$$\overline{F} = \prod_{i=0}^{3} (\overline{a}_1 + S_i) = \left[\overset{0}{\overset{/\!/}{\overline{a}_1}} + A + \overline{B} \right]\left[\overset{0}{\overset{/\!/}{\overline{a}_2}} + \overline{A} + B \right]$$

$$= (A + \overline{B})(\overline{A} + B)$$

since $\overline{a}_1 = \overline{a}_2 = 0$

A particular difficulty with using the notation in table 2-8 is the means of associating each S_i term with the corresponding a_i constant. This is because the actual S_i term used corresponds to the a_i terms which equal 0. A somewhat more convenient method is to use a shorthand notation for the product of *sums* (S_i) similar to the notation for sum of *products* (P_i). For instance, for the function in example 2.15, in the short form it is expressed as

$$F = \Sigma(1,2) = \overline{A}B + A\overline{B}$$

which lists the a_i terms which are 1. Similarly, we can also use a simplified form, such as

$$F = \prod(0,3) = (A + B)(\overline{A} + \overline{B})$$

which lists the S terms in which $a_i = 0$.

It then follows that the $\overline{F}$ function can be described by the remaining constants:

$$\overline{F} = \Sigma(0,3) = \overline{A}\,\overline{B} + AB$$

$$\overline{F} = \prod(1,2) = (A + \overline{B})(\overline{A} + B)$$

EXAMPLE 2.17

For the function $F = A + B$, express F and $\overline{F}$ with both P_i and S_i terms. By using the format of table 2-10, F can be described.

Table 2-10

a_i	P_i	S_i	$F = A + B$
a_0	$\overline{A}\,\overline{B}$	$A + B$	0
a_1	$\overline{A}B$	$A + \overline{B}$	1
a_2	$A\overline{B}$	$\overline{A} + B$	1
a_3	AB	$\overline{A} + \overline{B}$	1

Using the short notation

$$F = \Sigma(1,2,3) = \prod(0)$$

$$\overline{F} = \Sigma(0) = \prod(1,2,3)$$

Thus:

$$F = \underbrace{\overline{A}B}_{1} + \underbrace{A\overline{B}}_{2} + \underbrace{AB}_{3} = \underbrace{\left(A + B\right)}_{0}$$

$$\overline{F} = \underbrace{\overline{A}\,\overline{B}}_{0} = \underbrace{(A + \overline{B})}_{1}\underbrace{(\overline{A} + B)}_{2}\underbrace{(\overline{A} + \overline{B})}_{3}$$

2.5 BOOLEAN FUNCTIONS

By using the standard or canonical form, we now have a disciplined technique for analyzing Boolean functions. As a starting point, we will take the canonical standard sum for two variables

$$f(A,B) = a_0\overline{A}\,\overline{B} + a_1\overline{A}\,B + a_2 A\overline{B} + a_3 A B$$

In this case the number of a_i terms $t = 2^n = 2^2 = 4$. To determine the number of possible functions which can be generated for two variables, we note that a_i can only be 0 or 1, thus having only two combinations. Therefore,

$$2 \cdot 2 \cdot 2 \cdot 2 = 2^4 = 16$$

are the number of possible functions of two variables.

To find the number of functions of n variables, we simply note how many a_i factors are required in the standard form since the number of product terms will always be $t = 2^n$, and since each product term has only two combinations, then $2^t = (2)^{2^n}$ gives the number of functions of n variables.

For example, table 2-11 shows the number of functions for n as large as 4.

Table 2-11

n	$(2)^{2^n}$
1	4
2	16
3	256
4	65,536

From table 2-11 it is apparent that the case of $n = 2$, which is limited to 16 specific functions, is a very convenient group to examine. In fact, the characteristics of functions containing greater than two variables can be found in the two variable group.

Table 2-12

A	B	a_i	f_0	f_1	f_2	f_3	f_4	f_5	f_6	f_7	f_8	f_9	f_{10}	f_{11}	f_{12}	f_{13}	f_{14}	f_{15}
0	0	a_0	0	0	0	0	0	0	0	0	1	1	1	1	1	1	1	1
0	1	a_1	0	0	0	0	1	1	1	1	0	0	0	0	1	1	1	1
1	0	a_2	0	0	1	1	0	0	1	1	0	0	1	1	0	0	1	1
1	1	a_3	0	1	0	1	0	1	0	1	0	1	0	1	0	1	0	1

By setting up a table of all the possible 16 functions, each of the reduced functions can be obtained. This is shown in table 2-12.

$$f_0 = 0 \qquad\qquad\qquad f_8 = \overline{A}\,\overline{B} \rightarrow \text{NOR} = \overline{A + B}$$

$$f_1 = AB \qquad\qquad\qquad f_9 = \overline{A}\,\overline{B} + AB = \overline{A \oplus B}$$

$$f_2 = A\overline{B} \qquad\qquad\qquad f_{10} = \overline{B}$$

$$f_3 = A \qquad\qquad\qquad f_{11} = A + \overline{B}$$

$$f_4 = \overline{A}B \qquad\qquad\qquad f_{12} = \overline{A}$$

$$f_5 = B \qquad\qquad\qquad f_{13} = \overline{A} + B$$

$$f_6 = A \oplus B = A\overline{B} + \overline{A}B \qquad f_{14} = \overline{A} + \overline{B} \rightarrow \text{NAND} = \overline{A \cdot B}$$

$$f_7 = A + B \qquad\qquad\qquad f_{15} = 1$$

Functionally Complete Sets

Each function in table 2-12 has been expressed in terms of the three operators: $\cdot$, $+$, $-$. These operators as a group are a "functionally complete" set, in that they can describe all other functions. They are not, however, the only functionally complete set. Since we know that these three completely describe any Boolean function, then any other functions which perform the equivalent operations will also form a functionally complete set.

As an example, using our knowledge of De Morgan's theorem, we can state the following:

$$A \cdot B = \overline{\overline{A} + \overline{B}} \,,$$

$$A + B = \overline{\overline{A} \cdot \overline{B}}$$

This indicates that with the aid of the complement operator, $+$ and $\overline{A}$ can be substituted for $\cdot$, and also $\cdot$ and $\overline{A}$ can be substituted for $+$.

Table 2-13 shows how these substitutions are used to form two functionally complete sets.

Table 2-13

	Functionally Complete Sets	
Basic Operators	$A + B, \overline{A}$	$A \cdot B, \overline{A}$
$A \cdot B$	$\overline{\overline{A} + \overline{B}}$	$A \cdot B$
$A + B$	$A + B$	$\overline{\overline{A} \cdot \overline{B}}$
$\overline{A}$	$\overline{A}$	$\overline{A}$

EXAMPLE 2.18

Using only OR and NOT logic operations, show the logic diagram for the function

$$J = A \cdot \left[(B+C) \cdot \overline{D} + \overline{E} \cdot \overline{F} \right].$$

From table 2-13, the equivalent of $A \cdot B$ can be obtained as the logic shown in figure 2-48. Using this, the logic diagram for the function is shown in figure 2-49.

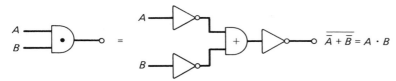

Figure 2-48 Equivalent AND Gate

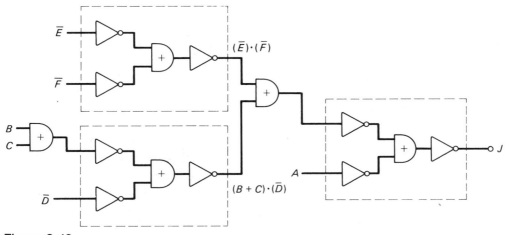

Figure 2-49

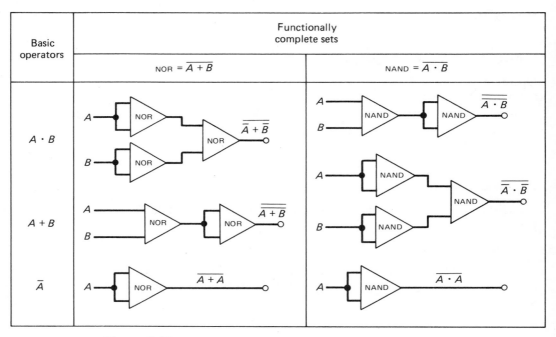

Figure 2-50

The AND operation, which is implementable by $\overline{\overline{A} + \overline{B}}$, can also be implemented by the operation $\overline{A + B}$, provided that the complement function ($\overline{A}$) is also available. This is logically a NOT OR operation, which is commonly labeled by the contraction NOR. Similarly, the $\overline{A \cdot B}$ operation, which is logically NOT AND is labeled NAND.

The NOR and NAND functions have the interesting characteristic that each is a functionally complete set by itself. This is because each has the capability of performing the equivalent of the three basic operators. These are shown in figure 2-50.

EXAMPLE 2.19

Using only NAND operators, show the logic diagram for $F = (A \cdot B + C)(D)$. The simplest way to do this is to use exact equivalents from figure 2-50. The AND and OR logic is shown in figure 2-51(a), with the NAND equivalents in figure 2-51(b). Note that the two logic inversions (see arrows) are redundant, and these two elements could be eliminated.

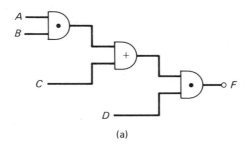

(a)

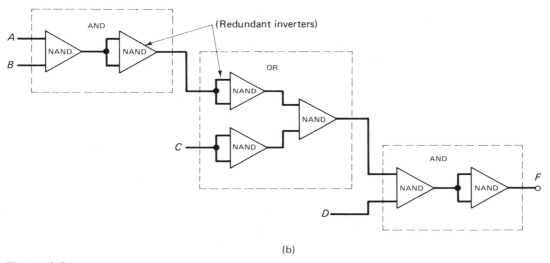

(b)

Figure 2-51

2.6 MINIMIZATION OF BOOLEAN FUNCTIONS

When three or more variables are contained in a Boolean function, the use of straightforward Boolean algebra becomes a rather cumbersome technique for minimization. The Karnaugh map is the more preferable method for guaranteeing that complete minimization is performed. Its usability extends up through five or six variables.

For a greater number of variables it is necessary to use other techniques, such as the Quine-McClusky method. This is a method for exhaustively comparing and tabulating all terms of the given function. Variations of tabular minimization techniques can be programmed on a digital computer for computer-aided reduction.

For general use, however, the Karnaugh map has undisputed value. Thus we will examine the maps in greater detail for use as one of the tools of the computer architect.

Three-Variable Maps

The three-variable Karnaugh map uses the same techniques that were described for two variables. That is, for a function such as

$$F = XYZ + XY\overline{Z}$$

the function can be factored as

$$F = XY\left(Z + \overline{Z} \right)$$
$$\underbrace{}_{1} \quad \underbrace{\phantom{\overline{Z}}}_{0}$$

This single-variable change is used to eliminate the Z variable, and is shown on the map as an adjacency.

To generate the map for three variables, we use the standard form as a starting point.

$$F(A,B,C) = a_0\overline{A}\,\overline{B}\,\overline{C} + a_1\overline{A}\,\overline{B}\,C + a_2\overline{A}\,B\overline{C} + a_3\overline{A}\,BC + a_4A\overline{B}\,\overline{C}$$

$$+ a_5A\overline{B}\,C + a_6AB\overline{C} + a_7ABC$$

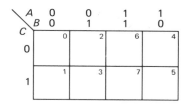

Figure 2-52

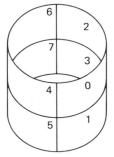

Figure 2-53

Using the terms in the standard form, a three-variable map can be constructed in which each cell has only a single-variable change between it and the next adjacent cell (figure 2-52). Each square (or cell) is labeled with the appropriate i subscript for each product term.

Note that there is a complete wraparound on the map, so that the cells on one end are actually adjacent to the other end (figure 2-53).

EXAMPLE 2.20

Using the function $f(X, Y, Z) = \Sigma(2, 3, 6, 7)$, reduce it both with map and algebraically using the identity $(X + \bar{X}) = 1$.

First, we will express F as a standard sum.

$$F = \underbrace{\bar{X}\,Y\bar{Z} + \bar{X}\,YZ} + \underbrace{XY\bar{Z} + XYZ}$$

The reduction can be broken into two steps, by using the first two terms, and then the last two. On the map, this function is shown in figure 2-54.

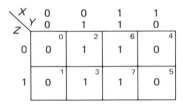

Figure 2-54

Step 1

To eliminate the first adjacency

$$F = \bar{X}\,Y\bar{Z} + \bar{X}\,YZ + XY\bar{Z} + XYZ$$

$$= \bar{X}\,Y(\bar{Z} + Z) + XY\bar{Z} + XYZ$$

$$= \bar{X}\,Y + XY\bar{Z} + XYZ$$

On the map, this is done as in figure 2-55.

Step 2

To eliminate the second adjacency

$$F = \bar{X}\,Y + XY\bar{Z} + XYZ$$

$$= \bar{X}\,Y + XY(\bar{Z} + Z)$$

On the map this is done in a like manner as shown in figure 2-56.

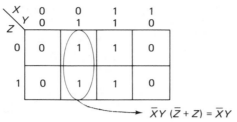

Figure 2-55

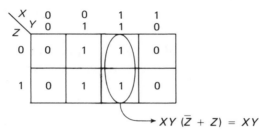

Figure 2-56

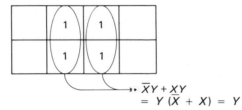

Figure 2-57

Step 3

The reduction can be taken one step farther, by taking into account the adjacency of the two reduced terms.

$$F = \overline{X}Y + XY$$

$$= Y(\overline{X} + X)$$

$$= Y$$

This is performed similarly in the map in figure 2-57.

The utility of the map is really demonstrated by examining the reduction of the four cells in one step as in figure 2-58. If we note that X has a variable change in the horizontal row and Z has a change in the vertical column, we can recognize that the only unchanged term is Y. With this type of visual inspection, a four-cell minimization will always occur. Because the minimization depends on adjacencies, minimized terms always require an even number of cells in a group.

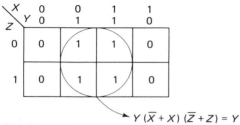

$$Y(\overline{X}+X)(\overline{Z}+Z)=Y$$

Figure 2-58

To aid in using the map, the types of groups encountered are summarized in figure 2-59.

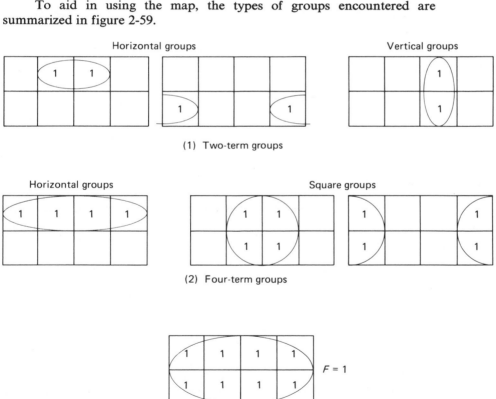

(1) Two-term groups

(2) Four-term groups

(3) Eight-term groups

Figure 2-59   Three Variable Groups

Four-Variable Maps

Four-variable maps are based on the standard form for four variables, in which the number of product terms are twice that contained in the three-variable form.

$$F(A,B,C,D) = a_0\overline{A}\,\overline{B}\,\overline{C}\,\overline{D} + a_1\overline{A}\,\overline{B}\,\overline{C}D + a_2\overline{A}\,\overline{B}\,C\overline{D} + a_3\overline{A}\,\overline{B}\,CD$$

$$= a_4\overline{A}\,B\overline{C}\,\overline{D} + a_5\overline{A}\,B\overline{C}D + a_6\overline{A}\,BC\overline{D} + a_7\overline{A}\,BCD$$

$$= a_8 A\overline{B}\,\overline{C}\,\overline{D} + a_9 A\overline{B}\,\overline{C}D + a_{10} A\overline{B}\,C\overline{D} + a_{11} A\overline{B}\,CD$$

$$= a_{12} AB\overline{C}\,\overline{D} + a_{13} AB\overline{C}D + a_{14} ABC\overline{D} + a_{15} ABCD$$

The map for $F(A,B,C,D)$ has the form shown in figure 2-60.

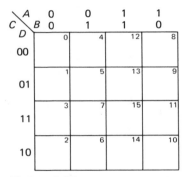

Figure 2-60

The types of groupings for minimization are summarized in figure 2-61.

EXAMPLE 2.21

Find the minimum function for the following:

(1) $F = \sum (0, 2, 8, 10, 11, 14, 15)$

(2) $G = \sum (0, 2, 3, 4, 6, 7, 15)$

1. F is shown in figure 2-62. The important consideration is to reduce as many variables as possible, which means the largest possible grouping. The grouping in figure 2-63 is logically equal to F, but it is not the maximum reduction. Figure 2-64, however, takes advantage of the largest grouping and results in the best minimization.

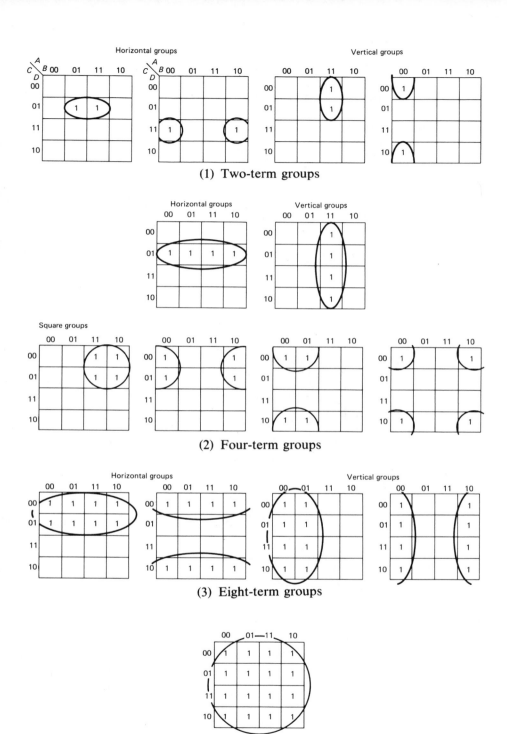

(1) Two-term groups

(2) Four-term groups

(3) Eight-term groups

$F(A, B, C, D) = 1$

(4) Sixteen-term group

Figure 2-61 Four Variable Groups

71

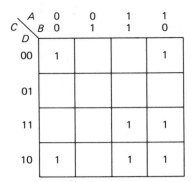

Figure 2-62

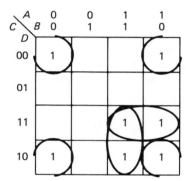

$\overline{B}\overline{D} + ACD + ABC$

Figure 2-63

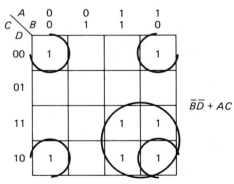

$\overline{B}\overline{D} + AC$

Figure 2-64

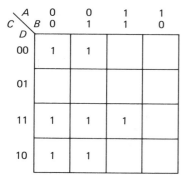

Figure 2-65

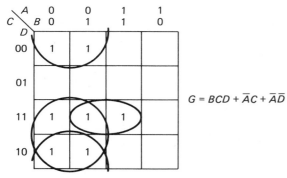

$G = BCD + \overline{A}C + \overline{A}\overline{D}$

Figure 2-66

2. G is shown in figure 2-65. In grouping terms, the single cells such as term 15 should first be grouped whenever possible. By looking for the largest groups, the minimization in figure 2-66 results.

Five-Variable Maps

The technique for five-variable maps requires using another dimension of adjacency. In figure 2-67 a five-variable map is shown as two *adjacent* four-variable maps, in which one represents the $\overline{A}$ map and the other the A map. Specifically, the map shows the adjacency of the 10-term and the 26-term groups, in which the $(\overline{A}+A)$ term is eliminated because of the adjacency.

For groups of terms, whenever there is an adjacency on both four-variable maps, the $(A+\overline{A})$ term will be eliminated. Thus all the group patterns for four variables can be extended to five variables. This is shown in figure 2-68 for two adjacent-term groups.

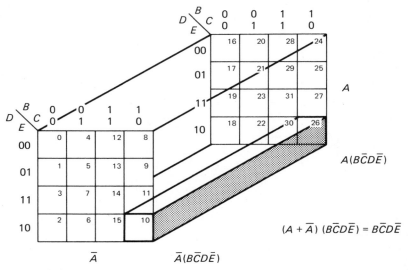

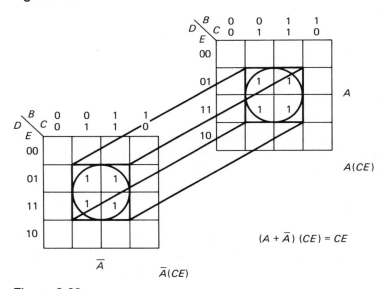

Figure 2-67

Figure 2-68

EXAMPLE 2.22

Simplify a function of five variables,

$$F(A,B,C,D,E) = \sum (1,3,17,19,24,26,28,30)$$

using a Karnaugh map.

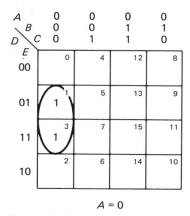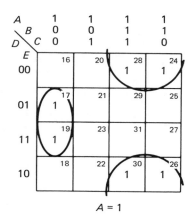

Figure 2-69

Figure 2-69 shows the function on a five-variable map.

On the $A = 1$ map, because the four-term group does not use $A = 0$, the resulting term is $AB\overline{E}$. The remaining term is common to $A = 1$ and $A = 0$. Therefore,

$$F(A, B, C, D, E) = AB\overline{E} + \overline{B}\,\overline{C}E$$

Unspecified Terms

A condition that can occur for a Boolean function is the case of having certain terms with unspecified values. This is usually the result of an imposed condition which states that a certain combination of variables will not occur or is not allowed to occur. An example of this is a circuit that recognizes binary inputs which are *binary coded decimal*, such as in figure 2-70.

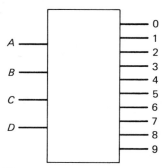

Figure 2-70

Table 2-14

Inputs				Output
A	B	C	D	
0	0	0	0	0
0	0	0	1	1
0	0	1	0	2
0	0	1	1	3
0	1	0	0	4
0	1	0	1	5
0	1	1	0	6
0	1	1	1	7
1	0	0	0	8
1	0	0	1	9
1	0	1	0	Unspecified
1	0	1	1	"
1	1	0	0	"
1	1	0	1	"
1	1	1	0	"
1	1	1	1	"

A typical application of this is a decimal display that is driven by binary inputs. At any instance the binary value is decoded to the appropriate decimal output line, using the values in table 2-14.

The characteristic of this application is that only ten of the sixteen possible combinations of A, B, C, D are used. Thus the binary valuations for decimal 10 to 15 are unspecified, because they are *not recognized* at the output. This situation can be used to advantage in some cases, as in the following example.

EXAMPLE 2.23

A circuit in which the inputs are binary coded decimal will present an output whenever the input values are decimal 4 or greater.

For this circumstance, the desired function is:

$$F = \sum (4, 5, 6, 7, 8, 9) + \sum_{\phi}(10, 11, 12, 13, 14, 15)$$

This states that decimal 4 to 9 are to be recognized, and that decimal 10 to 15 are "unspecified," since they are not defined for binary coded decimal. Note that the symbol ϕ is used to define the unspecified terms.

The map for F is shown in figure 2-71.

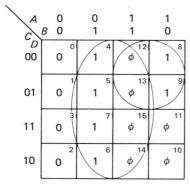

Figure 2-71

If the unspecified terms were not used, the result would be

$$F = \bar{A}B + A\bar{B}\bar{C}$$

However, if we use all the unspecified terms except 10 and 11 as ones, then

$$F = B + A\bar{C}$$

The increased simplification is quite evident in this instance. Additional examination would show that even this is not the minimum expression. Further reduction would result in $F = B + A$.

PROBLEMS

1. Prove the following by using the postulates:
   (a) Theorem 6
   (b) Theorem 7
   (c) Theorem 8
   (d) Theorem 9

2. Prove the following by using the basic theorems:
   (a) $(A + B)(B + C)(C + \bar{A}) = (A + B)(C + \bar{A})$
   (b) $AB + \bar{A}\bar{B} = A\bar{B} + \bar{A}B$
   (c) $\bar{A}\bar{B}\bar{C} + \bar{A}B\bar{C} + A\bar{B}C + AB\bar{C} + A\bar{B}\bar{C} = \bar{C} + A\bar{B}$
   (d) $\bar{A}\bar{C} + B\bar{C} + B + A\bar{B}\bar{C} + AC = \overline{\bar{A}BC}$
   (e) $\bar{A} + AC + A\bar{B}\bar{C} + AB\bar{C} + A\bar{B} + \bar{B}\bar{C} + A\bar{B} = 1$
   (f) $BC + \bar{A}\bar{B}\bar{C} + \bar{A}B\bar{C} + \bar{A}C = (\bar{A} + C)(\bar{A} + B)$

3. Use De Morgan's theorem to reduce the following:

    (a) $\overline{\overline{\overline{ABC}}\,(A+B)}$

    (b) $\overline{\overline{AC}+(\overline{AB}+C)(\overline{A}+C)}$

    (c) $\overline{(A+\overline{B})+(AB+\overline{AB})}$

    (d) $\overline{\left(\overline{AB}+\overline{A}+\overline{B}\right)+A}$

4. Draw a Venn diagram for the following:
    (a) $\overline{A}+\overline{B}+\overline{C}$
    (b) $AB+BC+C\overline{A}$
    (c) ABC
    (d) $A+AB$

5. Use the expansion theorem to obtain a standard sum:
    (a) $XY+ZY+\overline{Z}=f(X,Y,Z)$
    (b) $X+Y+\overline{Z}+W=f(X,Y,Z,W)$

6. Construct a truth table for the following:

    (a) $F=AB+C\overline{A}+BC$
    (b) $G=A+B+\overline{C}$
    (c) $H=AB+\overline{A}\overline{B}$
    (d) $J=A+BC$

7. Generate the canonical sum of products form for the functions in problem 6.

8. Repeat problem 7 for the product of sums form.

9. Show the relay switching circuits for the functions in problem 6.

10. Show the logic diagrams for the functions in problem 6.

11. Simplify (1) algebraically, and (2) with a Karnaugh map:
    (a) $\overline{A}\overline{B}\overline{C}D+A\overline{B}CD+\overline{A}\overline{B}C\overline{D}+A\overline{B}C\overline{D}=F$
    (b) $\overline{A}\overline{B}\overline{C}D+\overline{A}\overline{B}CD+\overline{A}B\overline{C}D+\overline{A}BCD=G$

12. Prove the following theorems using a Karnaugh map:
    (a) $AB+\overline{A}C+BC=AB+\overline{A}C$
    (b) $A\overline{B}=AB+\overline{A}\overline{C}+\overline{A}C$

13. For the functions in (11), determine the complements $\overline{F}$ and $\overline{G}$.

14. Obtain the simplest form of the following standard sums using a Karnaugh map:
    (a) $B=\Sigma(0,2,8,10)$
    (b) $K=\Sigma(1,5,7)+\Sigma_{\phi}(9,11)$
    (c) $J=\Sigma(1,3,5,7,10,11,14,15)+\Sigma_{\phi}(8,12)$
    (d) $G=\Sigma(0,4,2,6,8,9,10,11,12,14)$
    (e) $F=\Sigma(1,3,17,19,24,26,27)$

15. Find the simplest function for the maps in figure 2-72.

16. Simplify by any method:
    (a) $A \cdot [BC + CD + C + B + \overline{C}] + \overline{A}$
    (b) $\overline{A}B + \overline{B}C + A$

X \ Y	0 0	0 1	1 1	1 0
Z 0	1	1	1	1
1			1	

(a)

X \ Y	0 0	0 1	1 1	1 0
Z 0	1	1	1	1
1	1	1	1	1

(b)

X \ Y	0 0	0 1	1 1	1 0
Z 0	1			1
1		1		

(c)

Figure 2-72

Chapter 3

Register Structure

3.1 THE BASIC FLIP-FLOP

The register, as a basic microcomputer storage function, is made up of a collection of single bit storage elements. The primary form for this single bit storage is a device called a flip-flop. Its origins go back to vacuum tubes, where each of two tube amplifiers had their output signals fed back to the input of the other, so that depending on the input one amplifier always had a 1 output and the other a 0 (figure 3-1).

The fundamental operation of the flip-flop as a function with input and output is summarized in figure 3-2.

Basically, the set (S) input sets the output to a 1, whereas the reset (R) input resets the output to a 0. The complement of the output is always available as the output of the other amplifier in the pair.

In understanding the flip-flop, it is essential to think of it as a sequential device, in which we must be aware of the previous value of the flip-flop. Fortuitously, the flip-flop can be described by looking at the

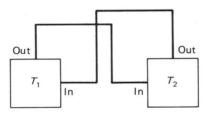

Figure 3-1

Inputs		Output
S	R	Q
1	0	1
0	1	0

Figure 3-2

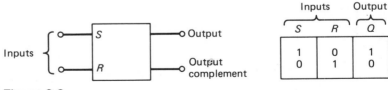

Figure 3-3

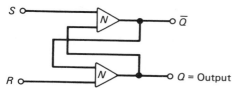

Figure 3-4

sequence of operations in a logic circuit consisting of NOT OR or NOR gates (figure 3-3).

These NOR gates are the solid state equivalent of their predecessor the vacuum tube circuit.

By using the configuration shown in figure 3-4, a flip-flop is obtained. Note that the output of each NOR is fed back to the input of the other NOR, which is the means for performing the storage function.

The Flip-Flop Operation

The operation of the flip-flop is explained by using a timing diagram in which the set (S), reset (R), and the flip-flop outputs ($Q, \overline{Q}$) are shown as logic levels graphed as a function of time intervals (figure 3-5). This diagram shows the effect of a new value of S or R applied to the input. By allowing a change at point a to occur, its effects are shown successively at point b and then at the output at point c. The state or condition of the flip-flop is sampled at the point $n + i$ where the effects of all changes are

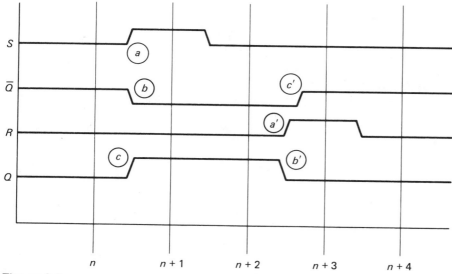

Figure 3-5

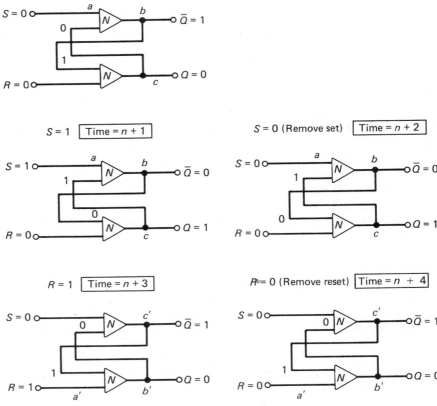

Figure 3-6

complete. A typical computer would have i as a clocked interval, in which a clock time would be selected such that all logic levels within the interval have settled to their final value.

The following explains each step performed in figure 3-6:

n (start): The starting conditions have $\overline{Q}=1$ and $Q=0$ as a stable condition with $S=R=0$.

$n+1$: After the n sample time, $S=1$ is applied at point a, which forces $\overline{Q}$ to be 0 at point b. Feeding the $\overline{Q}$ output to the second NOR, Q is forced to a 1 at point c. This 1 is fed back to the first NOR, changing that input from 0 to 1. The outputs are maintained at $Q=1$ and $\overline{Q}=0$ when sampled at $n+1$.

$n+2$: After $n+1$, the set is removed and the S input is now 0 at point a. However, the 1 input which is fed back from $Q=1$, maintains the first output at (b) at $\overline{Q}=0$. Thus, even when the set is removed, the flip-flop "remembers" the last input, and maintains (c) at the desired value of $Q=1$ during the $n+2$ interval.

$n+3$: $R=1$ is applied at (a'), which forces Q to 0 at (b'). This is fed to the first NOR, which changes $\overline{Q}$ to a 1 at (c'). Feeding the $\overline{Q}=1$ output back to the second NOR changes that input from 0 to 1. The output at (b') is maintained at $Q=0$ when examined at $n+3$.

$n+4$: The reset is removed at (a') and the R input is now 0. However, the $\overline{Q}=1$ input maintains the (b') output at 0. As was the case for the $S=1$ condition, when the reset is removed the flip-flop "remembers" because the 1 input fed back from (c') maintains the $Q=0$ condition at (b').

The S-R flip-flop has one specific restriction in its usage. If the logic of the NOR implementation is closely examined, it becomes evident that the simultaneous occurrence of both S and R results in rather unpredictable behavior. A race will occur to determine whether S or R is first, and of course that will be dependent on the switching speeds of each particular NOR. Because of this type of unpredictable behavior, this flip-flop is restricted to the case where S and R are never simultaneously 1.

Sampling Times

To clarify the way that time intervals are viewed, we can examine the timing diagram for the S-R flip-flop (figure 3-5). Our main concern is to determine what will result when a new input occurs. For example, at time n we have:

$$S=0$$

$$R=0$$

$$Q(n)=0$$

If an input value of $S=1$ is applied after sampling at n, the effect will not be evident until sampling at $n+1$:

$$S=1$$

$$R=0$$

$$Q(n+1)=1$$

Thus it is important that if S,R are specified to change immediately after a sample interval n, then the interval i between n and $n+1$ must be *long enough* to allow the effects of the change to be completed. This is

Table 3-1

S	R	$Q(n+1)$
0	0	$Q(n)$
0	1	0
1	0	1
1	1	ϕ

dependent on the maximum switching times of the NOR circuits used. Therefore, the "worst case" switching delay for a class of circuits *must* be known before a sample interval can be specified.

In table 3-1, the conditions are shown for the SR flip-flop in terms of sampled intervals. The use of ϕ for an unspecified output only appears when $S = R = 1$ are applied simultaneously. In table 3-1, n is used as the *present* sampling time, and $n+1$ as the *next* sample. These terms apply to the equivalent conditions in figure 3-5. However, this could also apply to any successive samples, such as $n+2$ or $n+3$. For the more general case, it is conventional to use $Q(n)$ for the present sample and $Q(n+1)$ for the next. Thus, in general,

$$Q(n+1) = f(Q(n), S, R) \qquad \text{(Eq. 3-1)}$$

The Clocked Flip-Flop

A guarantee of a proper sampling interval is systematically accomplished by "clocking" the flip-flop. This is done by predetermining a proper time interval $i = \Delta t$, and then generating a clock pulse T for sampling every interval (figure 3-7).

The width of T is usually small relative to Δt. For example, if $\Delta t = 400$ nanoseconds (one nanosecond $= 10^{-9}$ seconds), then the width of T would typically be less than 50 nanoseconds.

Note that for every Δt interval, $\Delta t_1 = \Delta t_2 = \Delta t_n$. This is the characteristic of a synchronous system. Asynchronous operation occurs when $\Delta t_1 \neq \Delta t_2 \neq \Delta t_n$, as in figure 3-8. This is typically a characteristic of input/output operations. However, within the structure of the microprocessor itself, all timing is synchronous.

The clocking of the SR flip-flop is performed as in figure 3-9.

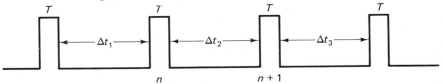

Figure 3-7

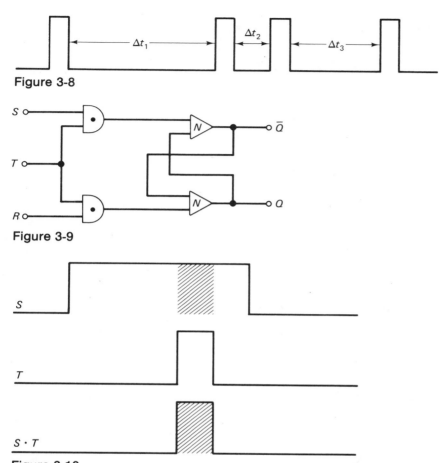

Figure 3-8

Figure 3-9

Figure 3-10

The T pulse is ANDed with S and with R, so that only the joint occurrence of T with a logic 1 input will appear as an input to the flip-flop (figure 3-10).

The logic of figure 3-9 can be more conveniently expressed as a single flip-flop element (figure 3-11). The clock is required as an additional input, with the gating of S and R performed internally.

Master-Slave Flip-Flop

A common flip-flop configuration in a computer application uses the output as inputs to the same or other flip-flops. This occurs when the flip-flops are temporarily storing data in successive operations. Figure 3-12

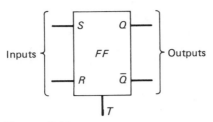

Figure 3-11

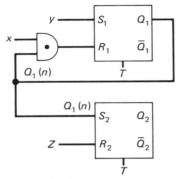

Figure 3-12

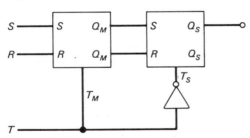

Figure 3-13

is an example of this where

$$Q_1(n+1) = f(S_1 = y, R_1 = x \cdot Q_1(n))$$

$$Q_2(n+1) = f(S_2 = Q_1(n), R_2 = Z)$$

Successful operation requires that the present outputs $Q(n)$ be immune to any input changes. The technique for accomplishing this uses a *master-slave* flip-flop, which is actually two separate flip-flops (figure 3-13), one the master, the other the slave. The difference between the two is determined by the level of the clock that is used. The master is clocked during the positive clock (T_M), which gates the S and R inputs. The slave

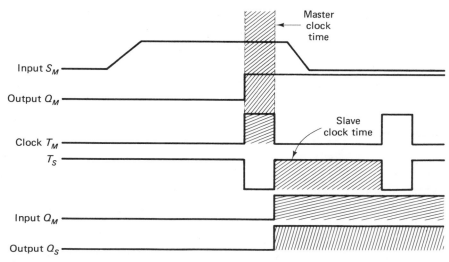

Figure 3-14

is clocked by the complemented clock (T_S), which occurs *after* the positive clock.

Figure 3-14 shows the effect of an $S=1$ input to the master. The output of the master, Q_M, becomes a 1 during the T_M clock interval. Although Q_M is used as the set input to the slave, the change is isolated since T_S, which is an inverted T_M, does not go positive until *after* the change to T_M has taken place. T_S is then used to gate the output of the master into the "set" input of the slave. Thus the isolation between input and output is maintained.

States

As a basic storage device, the flip-flop will always remember either of two binary states, 1 or 0. However, the flip-flop differs in the mechanism that *inputs* the data to be stored. In addition to the set-reset flip-flop, three other types of flip-flops are commonly used: (1) the D (for delay), (2) the τ (for toggle or complement), and (3) the JK, which is a variation of the SR.

The functioning of these different flip-flops can be completely described by using state diagrams. The state diagram is a technique for describing the states (or conditions) of a logic function.

By convention, states are diagramatically shown in a circle with the state symbol in the circle. For a flip-flop with only a 1 and 0 condition, there are only two states as shown in figure 3-15.

Figure 3-15

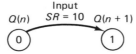

Figure 3-16

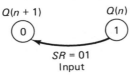

Figure 3-17

State changes will occur at distinct time intervals, in which the present state $Q(n)$ will change to the next state $Q(n+1)$.

$$Q(n) \rightarrow Q(n+1)$$

Since the states of a flip-flop are used to remember what is being presented to its input, then the next state must be a function of its present state and its input. This is functionally described as a more general variation of equation 3-1.

$$Q(n+1) = f(Q(n), \text{Input}) \tag{Eq. 3-2}$$

The transition from one state to another in the state diagram will depend on which state the flip-flop is presently in and which input occurs. For example, in a SR flip-flop, if the present state is 0, and $S=1, R=0$, then the flip-flop will be *set* to the 1 state (figure 3-16). Thus the arrow represents the state transition and "points" to the next state 1, which is $Q(n+1)$.

If the flip-flop is in the 1 state and the inputs are $S=0, R=1$, then the flip-flop will be reset with a transition to the 0 state (figure 3-17). In this case, 1 is $Q(n)$ and 0 is $Q(n+1)$.

A complete state diagram is shown in figure 3-18. It includes the condition in the zero state where $SR=00$ will do nothing, and $SR=01$ will

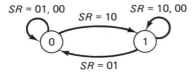

Figure 3-18

reset the flip-flop. Since the reset state 0 is the present state, then $Q(n+1)$ will equal $Q(n)$. A similar situation holds for the self-returning arrow at the 1 state.

State Equation

A general expression for the "next state" of any flip-flop can be obtained by using a Karnaugh map. The map is set up to follow the form of the functional equation for the state of the flip-flop, as in figure 3-19.

Each $Q(n+1)$ term can be evaluated by extracting *all* the state transitions from the state diagram and placing them on the map. The result is the state equation for the flip-flop. Using this approach, we will obtain the state equations for the four major flip-flop types.

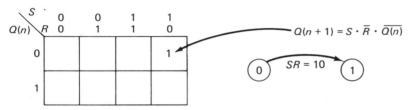

$$Q(n+1) = S \cdot \bar{R} \cdot \overline{Q(n)}$$

Figure 3-19   Map for $Q(n+1)$

The Set-Reset Flip-Flop

By using the state diagram for the *SR* flip-flop in figure 3-18, the Karnaugh map for the flip-flop states can be obtained (figure 3-20).

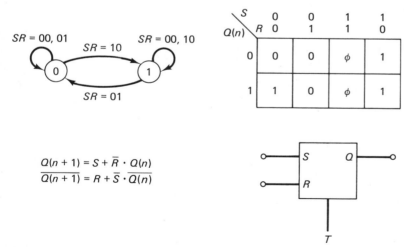

$$Q(n+1) = S + \bar{R} \cdot Q(n)$$
$$\overline{Q(n+1)} = R + \bar{S} \cdot \overline{Q(n)}$$

Figure 3-20   The *SR* Flip-Flop

Note that when $SR = 11$, these are not allowed, so that they become "unspecified" terms. Thus they can be appropriately treated as having an optional valuation, φ. The equations for $Q(n+1)$ from the map have taken this into account.

JK Flip-Flop

A difficulty with the SR flip-flop is the ambiguity that can occur if S and R ever occur coincidentally. The JK flip-flop is a solution in which the SR flip-flop is modified to define the condition of $J = K = 1$.

Specifically, this condition defines a toggle operation for the flip-flop, in which $Q(n+1) = \overline{Q(n)}$ whenever $JK = 11$. This is implemented by the addition of logic to the inputs of an SR flip-flop, as shown in figure 3-21. The JK inputs are modifying the SR inputs such that:

$$S = J\overline{Q} \quad \text{and} \quad R = KQ$$

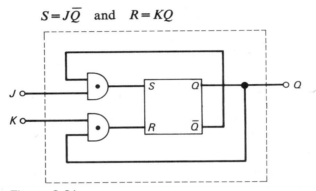

Figure 3-21

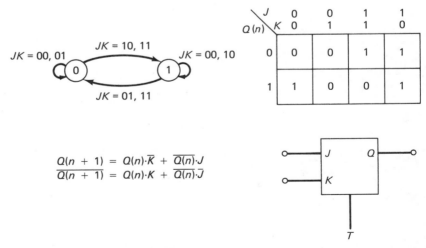

$$Q(n + 1) = Q(n) \cdot \overline{K} + \overline{Q(n)} \cdot J$$
$$\overline{Q(n + 1)} = Q(n) \cdot K + \overline{Q(n)} \cdot \overline{J}$$

Figure 3-22   The JK Flip-Flop

The state equations are obtained from the map of $Q(n+1)$, as shown in figure 3-22.

In the state design and the map, the only difference between the JK and the SR is, of course, the $JK=11$ condition.

The D Flip-Flop

The D flip-flop is a variation of the JK in which a *single* input (D) is used to store data (figure 3-23). The next state is always determined by the input, so that $Q(n+1)=D$.

The state diagram for the D flip-flop is shown in figure 3-24. For the D flip-flop, the state map is simply a demonstration of the statement that the next state always follows the input.

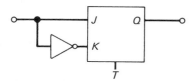

Figure 3-23

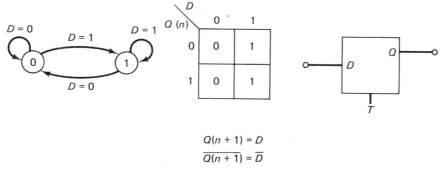

$$Q(n + 1) = D$$
$$\overline{Q(n + 1)} = \overline{D}$$

Figure 3-24   The D Flip-Flop

The τ Flip-Flop

The characteristics of the JK flip-flop are used to form a τ flip-flop, which is another single input storage device (figure 3-25). By tying together the JK inputs, the toggle function will always be performed.

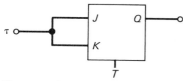

Figure 3-25

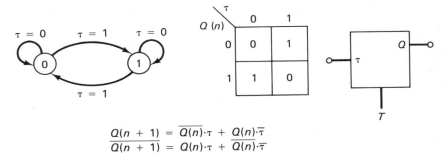

$$Q(n + 1) = \overline{Q(n)} \cdot \tau + Q(n) \cdot \overline{\tau}$$
$$\overline{Q(n + 1)} = Q(n) \cdot \tau + \overline{Q(n)} \cdot \overline{\tau}$$

Figure 3-26   The τ Flip-Flop

This configuration is quite effective when the flip-flops are grouped to form a binary counter. The state diagram and the resulting equations are shown in figure 3-26.

EXAMPLE 3.1

A variation of a *SR* flip-flop is defined as having a *third* input τ which performs a complement (or toggle) operation. The condition for a *SR* flip-flop in which $SR \neq 1$, will hold for this flip-flop. Also, τ can never occur whenever S or R equals 1, so that $\tau S = \tau R = 0$ will always hold.

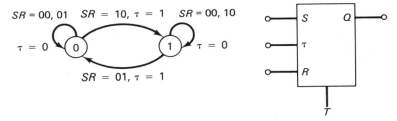

Figure 3-27

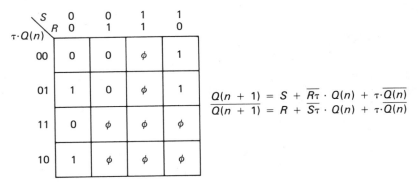

$$Q(n + 1) = S + \overline{R\tau} \cdot Q(n) + \tau \cdot \overline{Q(n)}$$
$$\overline{Q(n + 1)} = R + \overline{S\tau} \cdot Q(n) + \tau \cdot \overline{Q(n)}$$

Figure 3-28

Determine the state equations for the $SR\tau$ flip-flop. The flip-flop and its state diagram are shown in figure 3-27.

The state diagram is converted to a Karnaugh map in figure 3-28 and the equations are taken from the map. Because of the constraint that S and R can never occur when $\tau = 1$, these conditions are mapped as unspecified terms (ϕ).

3.2 REGISTER OPERATIONS

The storage register in a microprocessor performs a very central role because it is the interim storage for the logic operations that make things work. In particular, the operations in a processor will occur *between* clock pulses, as shown in figure 3-29.

The clock pulse that *follows* each operation is used to gate the results of the operation into the flip-flops that form the selected register. In figure 3-30, the results of operation A are stored in a register at the occurrence of the clock, so that the results of the operation are available to be used by operation B, the next successive operation. Associated with each register is a collection of logic that is dedicated to perform the required register operation, as in figure 3-30.

The following sections describe the logic for performing various types of register operations.

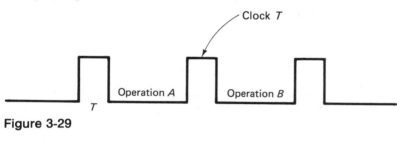

Figure 3-29

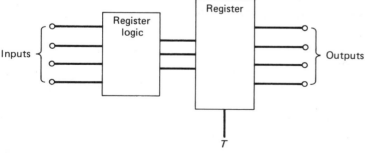

Figure 3-30

Data Transfer

The storage of data in a register requires the transfer of data into the register from some source, usually another register. The mechanism for performing the transfer uses two inputs into the register: (1) the data to be stored, and (2) the *enable* or control input, which allows the data input to be transferred in a scheduled manner (figure 3-31).

The actual logic for the data transfer is an expanded version of that used in each individual flip-flop. Figure 3-32 shows the logic levels versus time for the inputs to the flip-flop. Note that the data is not clocked into the flip-flop until the enable signal is present *coincident* with a clock.

Using a clocked D flip-flop, in figure 3-33 the data from register B is transferred into register A. The logic equation for the parallel transfer is $D_i = B_i \cdot [\text{Enable}]$. To avoid a cluttered drawing, most examples shown will describe only 3 bits of the register.

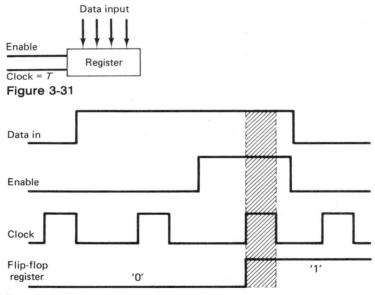

Figure 3-31

Figure 3-32

Shift Operations

The position of binary data in a register is modified by the shift operation. This operation is used for scaling numerical values by a factor of 2 or for positioning groups of data. For example, a data field of (00000010) can be multiplied by a factor of 2 by shifting one position to the left (00000100). This left shift operation is implemented as in figure 3-34 for 3 bits.

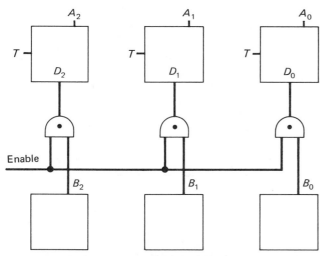

Figure 3-33   Data Transfer from Register *B* to Register *A*

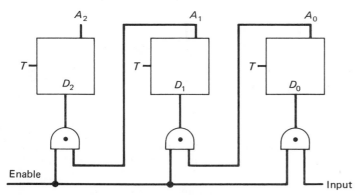

Figure 3-34   Register Shift Left

The logic equation for the operation is $D_i = A_{i-1} \cdot [\text{Enable}]$. A right shift operation can be similarly implemented, as shown in figure 3-35. The logic equation for a right shift is $D_i = A_{i+1} \cdot [\text{Enable}]$.

Note that the *input* can be selected to accommodate the type of operation. For a *logical* right shift, the input is 0, so that (101) becomes (010). However, if an arithmetic shift is performed, the sign bit, which is the leftmost bit, is used at the input. Thus, for an arithmetic right shift, (101) becomes (110).

Serial Data Transfer

Serial data transfer is performed when data is presented 1 bit at a time to a register. This type of operation occurs when a serial input device

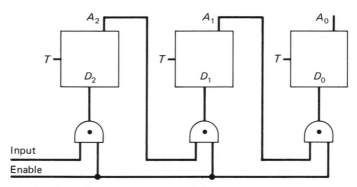

Figure 3-35   Register Shift Right

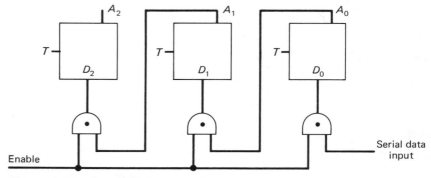

Figure 3-36   Serial Data Input

transfers data into a computer. The operation is identical to the shift operation, except that the input line is supplied by the serial data input as shown in figure 3-36.

In this instance, the logic equations are

$$D_i = A_{i-1} \cdot [\text{Enable}]$$

$$D_0 = \text{Input} \cdot [\text{Enable}]$$

The data transfer can be a left or right shift operation, depending on whether the left or right side of the input data is first entered.

Register Modification

In addition to storing new data in a register, it is often convenient to modify the existing register contents, including such operations as logical complement. In this instance, a bit pattern such as (011) would be changed to (100). The register structure that performs this is shown in figure 3-37.

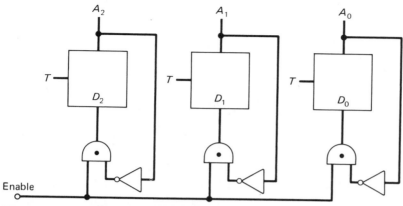

Figure 3-37 Register Complement

The logical equation for the complement is

$$D_i = \overline{A_i} \cdot [\,\text{Enable}\,]$$

Other operations that modify the register include performing such Boolean logic operations as AND. For example, if the register contains (011) and the input function is (001) then the following takes place:

$$A_i = (011)$$

$$\underline{In_i = (001)}$$

$$In_i \cdot A_i = (001)$$

This operation is performed by the configuration in figure 3-38. The logic equation for the operation is:

$$D_i = A_i \cdot In_i \cdot [\,\text{Enable}\,]$$

Similarly, the logic OR would be as in the following example:

$$A_i = (101)$$

$$\underline{In_i = (001)}$$

$$In_i + A_i = (101)$$

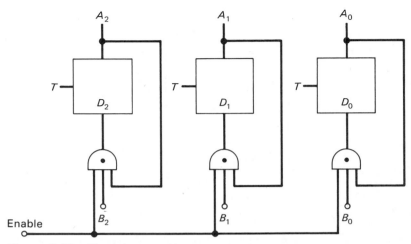

Figure 3-38   Register AND

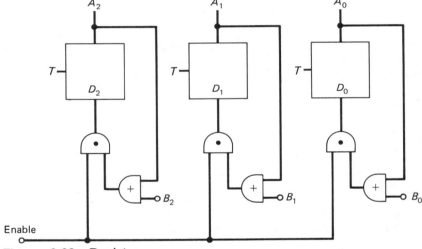

Figure 3-39   Register OR

This logic OR is shown in the register structure in figure 3-39. The logic equation for the OR operation is:

$$D_i = (A_i + In_i) \cdot [\,\text{Enable}\,]$$

Counters

A very basic function in a computer is the counting operation, which is the most primitive arithmetic operation. Very early in the days of structuring

Table 3-2   3-Bit Binary Counter States

Decimal	Binary
0	000
1	001
2	010
3	011
4	100
5	101
6	110
7	111
8	000

electronic computers, techniques were evolved for combining register storage with logic gates to construct a counter. The techniques utilized the characteristics of binary numbers as they perform the counting function. Table 3-2 lists a 3-bit counter, showing the binary state for each count.

Table 3-2 shows the characteristics of the two-valued binary numbers, in which we can only count up to 1, and then must proceed to the next higher position. For example, in the decimal system we count from 0 to 9 in the units column, but after the number 9 we zero the units and record a 1 in the tens column (table 3-3).

Table 3-3   Decimal Sequence

Decimal
00
01
02
03
04
05
06
07
08
09
10

Table 3-4   Binary Sequence

Binary
00
01
10

Similarly, in binary, which only can go as far as 1, after the 1 we zero the units and record a 1 in the twos column (table 3-4).

Thus we see that the following occurs:

1. The units column complements *every* time there is a "count" input (table 3-5).

Table 3-5   Binary Sequence

000		
001 ←	⎫	Units
010 ←	⎪	column
011 ←	⎪	change
100 ←	⎬	for every
101 ←	⎪	new count
110 ←	⎪	
111 ←	⎭	

2. The twos column complements *every* time the previous lower-order ones column goes to its maximum of 1 (table 3-6).

Table 3-6   Binary Sequence

000	
001	
010	←
011	
100	←
101	
110	←
111	

3. The fours column complements *every* time the two previous lower-order columns go to their maximum of 11 (table 3-7).

Table 3-7   Binary Sequence

000	
001	
010	
011	
100	←
101	
110	
111	
000	←

Counter Equations

From the preceding, we can generate the equations for the logic which will configure a register as a counter. Assume that the enable input is a signal called "count." Also, since the change in states for the flip-flops require complementation, it is evident that τ flip-flops are most appropriate.

Initial Conditions: The register will be "cleared," so that an initial state of (000) will be guaranteed.

A_0: The least significant bit will be complemented whenever the "count" enable occurs. Thus the input equation for the least significant bit in the counter is

$$\tau_0 = \text{count}$$

A_1: The twos position will be complemented whenever the lower order A_0 has a value of $A_0 = 1$ at the time the "count" enable occurs. Thus

$$\tau_1 = A_0 \cdot \text{count}$$

A_2: The fours position will be complemented whenever the lower-order bits $A_1 A_0 = 11$ and the "count" enable occurs. Thus

$$\tau_2 = A_1 A_0 \cdot \text{count}$$

It should be evident that this approach can be extrapolated to all higher-order stages for larger counters. The structure of this counter is shown in figure 3-40.

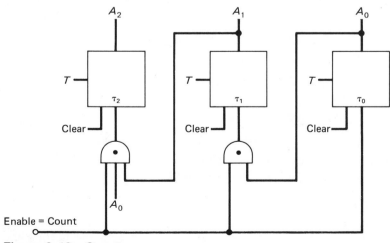

Figure 3-40   Counter

Table 3-8   Altered Count

		A_2	A_1	A_0
	0	0	0	0
	1	0	0	1
	2	0	1	0
	3	0	1	1
	4	1	0	0
	5	1	0	1
Normal Count	6	(1	1	0)
Desired Count	0	0	0	0

Normal Count Transition			Desired Count Transition		
1	0	1	1	0	1
↓	↓	↓	↓	↓	↓
1	1	0	0	0	0
A_2	A_1	A_0	A_2	A_1	A_0

Altered Counts

The situation often arises where a count sequence is desired that does *not* form some multiple of 2. For example, to obtain a count of 5, it is necessary to use a three-stage counter that recycles at 6 before the full cycle count is reached (table 3-8).

Two conditions are required to modify the counter structure:

1. *A* level (A_i) must be presented as an *output* to signal the occurrence of the 5 count. The first condition, the occurrence of (101), is obtained by gating the 5-count state.

   $$5 \text{ count} = A_2 \overline{A_1} A_0$$

2. The *count transition* from $5 = (101)$ to $6 = (110)$ must be altered to a transition from

   $$5 = (101) \quad \text{to} \quad 0 = (000)$$

   This second condition (forcing a (000)) requires the addition of a modifying condition to the count sequence. This is obtained by examining the state transition for each bit position.

Equations for Altered Count

A_0: Since the transition from $1 \rightarrow 0$ is the same for both the normal and the desired count, then $\tau_0 = \text{count}$.

A_1: In this instance the normal count ($\tau_1 = A_0 \cdot$[count]) is to be *inhibited* from toggling when a 5 count is present. Thus

$$\tau_1 = (A_0 \cdot [\text{count}]) \cdot \overline{(5\ \text{counts})}$$

A_2: This case requires an *additional* toggling for the case of a 5 count.

$$\tau_2 = (A_0 A_1 \cdot [\text{count}] + \overbrace{(5\ \text{count}) \cdot [\text{count}]}^{\text{addition term}}$$

$$\tau_2 = (A_0 A_1 + (5\ \text{count})) \cdot [\text{count}]$$

$$= (A_0 A_1 + A_0 \overline{A}_1 A_2) \cdot [\text{count}]$$

Thus the technique depends on whether the desired transition and the normal transition are the same, such that (1) there is no change in transition; or (2) the normal toggle must be *inhibited* from occurring at the transition time; or (3) a toggle must be *forced* to occur at the transition time. These conditions are summarized below:

1. *No change in transitions*

Normal		Desired		Modification
$0 \to 1$		$0 \to 1$		
$1 \to 0$	$=$	$1 \to 0$		None
$0 \to 0$		$0 \to 0$		$\tau_i = (A_{i-1} \cdot A_{i-2} \cdots) \cdot [\text{count}]$
$1 \to 1$		$1 \to 1$		

2. *Inhibit toggle at transition*

Normal	Desired	Modification
$0 \to 1$	$0 \to 0$	
$1 \to 0$	$1 \to 1$	$\tau_i = (A_{i-1} \cdot A_{i-2} \cdots) \cdot [\text{count}] \cdot \overline{(\text{Last count})}$

INHIBIT TERM

3. *Forced toggle at transition*

Normal	Desired	Modification
$1 \to 1$	$1 \to 0$	$\tau_i = (A_{i-1} \cdot A_{i-2} \cdots) \cdot [\text{count}]$
$0 \to 0$	$0 \to 1$	$+ (\text{Last count}) \cdot [\text{count}]$

FORCING TERM

The structure for the 5 counter is shown in figure 3-41.

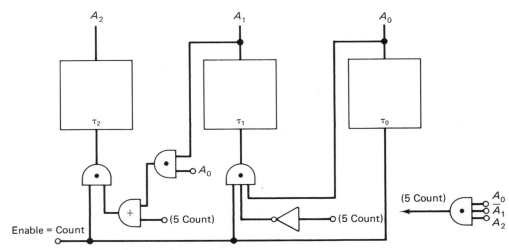

Figure 3-41   5 Counter

EXAMPLE 3.2

To obtain a binary version of a decimal counter, a binary-coded-decimal code (or BCD) is used. This is simply a 4-stage counter in which the count is recycled after the count of $9=(1001)$, rather than completing the full cycle of $15=(1111)$. Show the register structure for a BCD counter.

Table 3-9 shows the BCD count. The counter can be configured by using a normal count sequence that will be modified when a 9 count occurs.

Table 3-9   BCD Sequence

Decimal		A_3	A_2	A_1	A_0
	0	0	0	0	0
	1	0	0	0	1
	2	0	0	1	0
	3	0	0	1	1
	4	0	1	0	0
	5	0	1	0	1
	6	0	1	1	0
	7	0	1	1	1
	8	1	0	0	0
	9	1	0	0	1
Normal Count	10	(1	0	1	0)
Desired Count	0	(0	0	0	0)

A_0: There is no difference between *normal* and *desired*, so that

$$\tau_0 = [\text{count}]$$

A_1: This transition is normally $0 \rightarrow 1$, but a $0 \rightarrow 0$ is required. Thus the toggle must be inhibited at a count of 9.

$$(\text{count} = 9) = A_3 \overline{A}_2 \overline{A}_1 A_0$$

and

$$\tau_1 = A_0 (\overline{\text{count} = 9}) \cdot [\text{count}]$$

A_2: No change is required, so that

$$\tau_2 = A_0 A_1 \cdot [\text{count}]$$

A_3: A $1 \rightarrow 1$ transition must be replaced by $1 \rightarrow 0$, thus

$$\tau_3 = (A_2 A_1 A_0 + (\text{count} = 9)) \cdot [\text{count}]$$

The BCD counter is shown in figure 3-42.

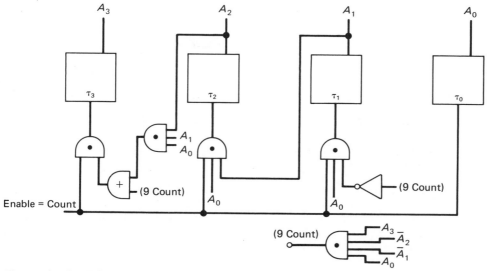

Figure 3-42   BCD Counter

Superposition

Most typically, a register structure for a microcomputer requires more than one type of register operation. This is obtained by superimposing the appropriate operation with the corresponding *enable*. The characteristic of the enable control is that of mutual exclusivity—that is, only one enable would be expected to occur at any one time, since it would usually lead to unpredictable results if, for instance, such operations as shift and complement were attempted during the same time interval. Thus, when superimposing operations, it can be assumed that only one particular enable is allowed.

The superposition operation will have the following pattern for each register stage:

$$D = \text{In}_B \cdot \text{Enab}_B + \text{In}_C \cdot \text{Enab}_C + \cdots \text{In}_n \cdot \text{Enab}_n$$

Thus the logic mechanism of ORing the separate functions allows the combining to take place, as shown in figure 3-43.

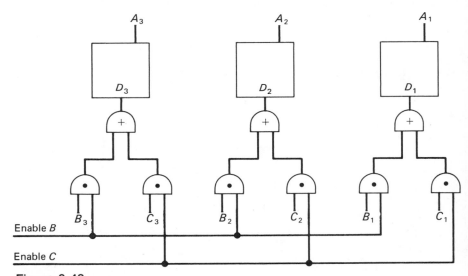

Figure 3-43

EXAMPLE 3.3

Show a shift register that performs both left and right shifts. By using the technique of figure 3-43, the left and right shifts are superimposed in figure 3-44 with the following input equation:

$$D_i = [\text{RtShEn}] \cdot A_{i+1} + [\text{LtShEn}] \cdot A_{i-1}$$

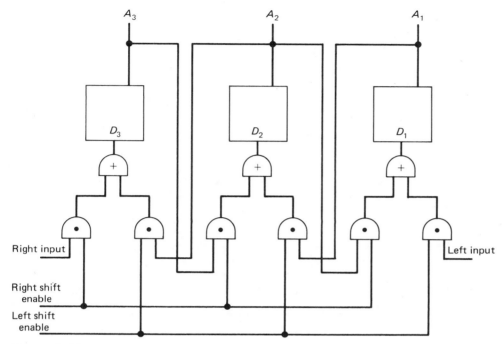

Figure 3-44

EXAMPLE 3.4

Show a register A that accepts either a parallel transfer from B, or a logical OR of A with B. By using the superposition principal, the desired structure will take the form shown in figure 3-45:

$$D_i = B_i \cdot [\text{ParEn}] + (A_i + B_i) \cdot [\text{OrEn}]$$

EXAMPLE 3.5

Using JK flip-flops, superimpose a logical right shift and a binary counter in a *two*-stage register. The proper approach to this logical structure is to obtain the equations separately for each of the two operations in terms of JK flip-flops. The superposition is accomplished by the logical OR of each J and K.

For the logical right shift, the operation is first configured in the manner previously described using a D flip-flop (figure 3-46).

To use a JK flip-flop to perform the shift, the JK equivalent of the D flip-flop is substituted in figure 3-47. This requires that the equations for the equivalent J and K inputs are obtained first, and then ANDed with the enable.

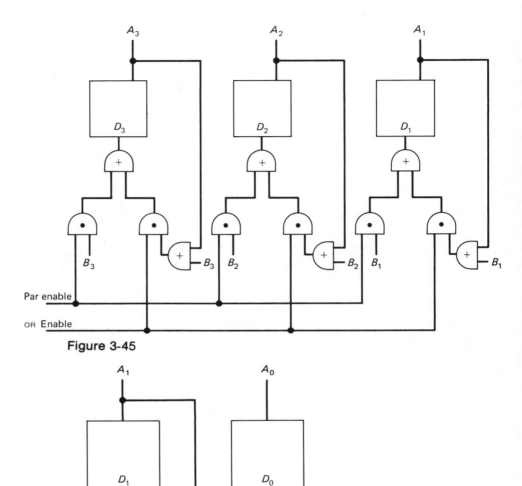

Figure 3-45

Figure 3-46

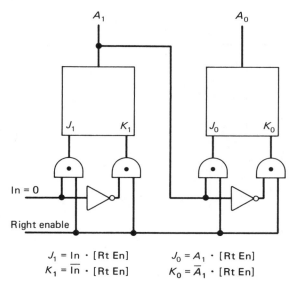

$$J_1 = \text{In} \cdot [\text{Rt En}] \qquad J_0 = A_1 \cdot [\text{Rt En}]$$
$$K_1 = \overline{\text{In}} \cdot [\text{Rt En}] \qquad K_0 = \overline{A}_1 \cdot [\text{Rt En}]$$

Figure 3-47

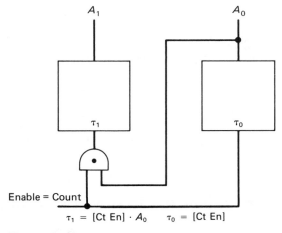

$$\tau_1 = [\text{Ct En}] \cdot A_0 \qquad \tau_0 = [\text{Ct En}]$$

Figure 3-48

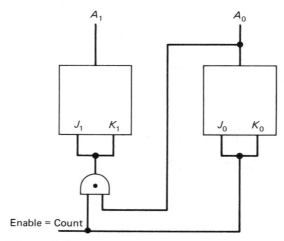

Figure 3-49

For the binary counter operation, figure 3-48 shows the previously described τ flip-flop configurations.

$$\tau_0 = [\,\text{count}\,]$$

$$\tau_1 = A_0 \cdot [\,\text{count}\,]$$

As was done for the shift operation, the τ flip-flop is converted to a JK equivalent in figure 3-49.

$$\begin{cases} J_0 = [\,\text{count}\,] \\ K_0 = [\,\text{count}\,] \end{cases}$$

$$\begin{cases} J_1 = A_0 \cdot [\,\text{count}\,] \\ K_1 = A_0 \cdot [\,\text{count}\,] \end{cases}$$

The superposition can now be performed by combining the JK equations for both operations:

$$J_0 = [\,\text{count}\,] + A_1 [\,\text{Rt En}\,]$$

$$K_0 = [\,\text{count}\,] + \overline{A}_1 [\,\text{Rt En}\,]$$

$$J_1 = A_0 [\,\text{count}\,] + \text{In} \cdot [\,\text{Rt En}\,]$$

$$K_1 = A_0 [\,\text{count}\,] + \overline{\text{In}} \, [\,\text{Rt En}\,]$$

The logic diagram that implements the superimposed equations is shown in figure 3-50.

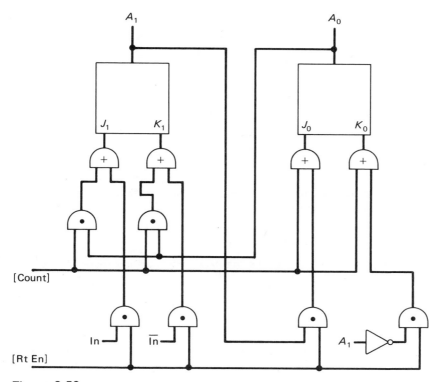

Figure 3-50

PROBLEMS

1. Diagram a *JK* master-slave flip-flop using only *SR* flip-flops and logic gates.

2. Show a *D* flip-flop configured from a *SR* flip-flop and logic gates.

3. A register *B* in a computer consists of two *D*-type flip-flops, B_1 and B_0.
   (a) A serial input *I* is presented to the register so that data is serially transferred as a right shift operation into *B*. The serial enable signal is RSH. Write the input equations for D_1 and D_0.
   (b) If an input *J* is entered as a left shift, write the equations for D_1 and D_0. The serial enable is LSH.
   (c) For a parallel loading of *B* from a register *C* (also 2 bits wide), write the equations for D_1 and D_0. The parallel enable is PLD.
   (d) The register *B* can also be configured for serial or parallel inputs. Show the D_1 and D_0 equations for the case in which *both* the left shift in (b) and the parallel load from *B* in (c) occur.
   (e) Show the equations for D_1 and D_0 in which an enable BCMP will allow the contents of *B* to be complemented, and another enable CCMP will load the complement of register *C* into *B*.

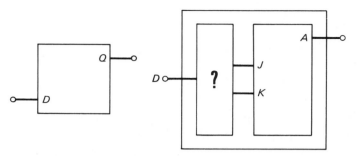

Figure 3-51

4. The input to a D flip-flop is $D = A\bar{B} + C\bar{B}D$. Use a JK flip-flop to perform in an equivalent functional manner. See figure 3-51.

5. Design a binary counter in which the highest count is 6. If a seventh count occurs, the counter will recycle to zero.

6. Design a two-stage binary counter that both counts up and counts down.

Chapter 4

Clocked Sequential Logic

The basic operations in a microcomputer are all performed in a time-sequential manner. Each operation follows a scheduled time sequence, which must be completely defined. The technique for designing time-dependent logic circuits uses a disciplined method called *sequential circuit synthesis*. The following sections examine the synthesis process, beginning with a state diagram and resulting in the final logic circuit.

4.1 THE GENERAL MODEL

The basic clocked sequential machine is one in which events in time are sampled at discrete intervals. The control of the machine is determined by its present state. The state is the memory that keeps track of just where the machine is in a sequence of events.

The states of the machine and its output are functionally described as

$$Q(n+1) = f(Q(n), \text{Input})$$

$$\text{Output} = Z = g(Q(n), \text{Input})$$

where $Q(n)$ is the machine state at time n.

As a clocked system, the sampled time n will occur at successive clocked times. A general model for a clocked sequential machine is shown in figure 4-1.

Note that this is simply a description of a logic implementation of the equations for $Q(n+1)$ and Z. The output is obtained by examining the input and $Q(n)$. The next state $Q(n+1)$ is not a separate circuit entity from $Q(n)$, but simply the *value* that the $Q(n)$ storage element will take in the next time interval. Thus, the input to the state memory is not $Q(n+1)$, but

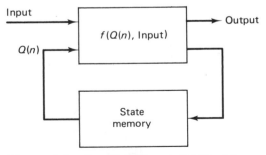

Figure 4-1   General Sequential Model

the logic that will cause the state memory to change. The following example is a clarification of this concept.

EXAMPLE 4.1

Using a two-stage binary counter, (1) show the state diagram, and (2) describe the logic, using the general sequential model.

1. The state diagram for a counter is quite uncomplicated (figure 4-2). It is only dependent on a single input, the count enable, which we will refer to as (Ct).
2. A two-stage counter is shown in figure 4-3 in the same form as in chapter 3.

Since y_0 and y_1 represent the state memory, a minor reconfiguration will show the counter as a generalized sequential machine (figure 4-4).

It is evident here that τ_0 and τ_1 are the next state generators. That is, the inputs to τ_i determine what the transition from $Q_i(n)$ to $Q_i(n+1)$ will be (figure 4-5). It should also be noted that the combinations of $y_0 y_1$

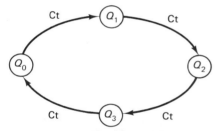

Figure 4-2   Counter State Diagram

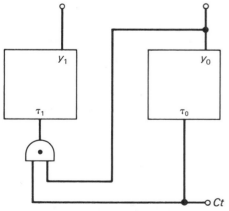

Figure 4-3   Two-Stage Counter

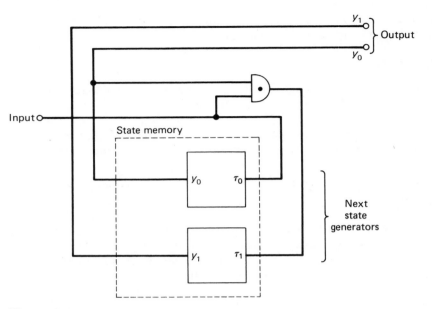

Figure 4-4

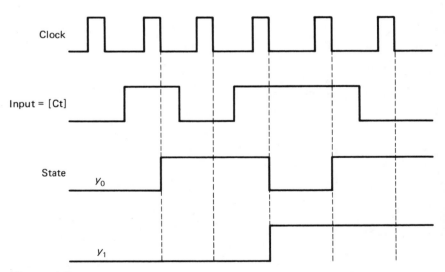

Figure 4-5

define the states for this example. That is

$$Q_0 = \bar{y}_1 \bar{y}_0$$

$$Q_1 = \bar{y}_1 y_0$$

$$Q_2 = y_1 \bar{y}_0$$

$$Q_3 = y_1 y_0$$

The timing for the two-stage counter is shown in figure 4-5 for a random occurrence of inputs.

4.2 STATE DESCRIPTIONS

The beginning point for sequential logic synthesis is the state diagram. This is a graphical means of describing all the possible occurrences in a sequential circuit. Once described, then the transition from state diagram to logic circuit can be performed by a progression of defined steps.

In the previous discussions of state diagrams as used for flip-flops, the generation of an output condition was not considered, since only the state of the memory element was discussed. For an *input/output* sequential machine, in addition to controlling the machine states, a separate output must occur when defined conditions have been met. In the previous example, a counter was used as a tutorial clarification of a sequential machine structure. For the counter, the *states* are the *outputs*. These are classified as "level" outputs.

Clocked outputs, the present subject, occur before and sometimes after the clock pulse, but are specifically valid for the time duration of the clock pulse. This is, of course, provided that the appropriate level input and level state conditions are present. These conditions thus satisfy the

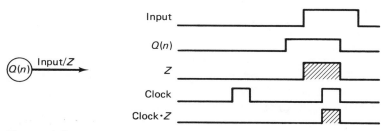

Figure 4-6

functional equation

$$Z = \text{Output} = g(Q(n), \text{Input})$$

The state diagram in figure 4-6 represents this condition.

The following examples demonstrate the use of state diagrams to represent input/output clocked sequential logic.

EXAMPLE 4.2

An output Z will be generated in a sequential circuit whenever, given an initial zero, a sequence of three ones is followed by a zero (figure 4-7).

Figure 4-7

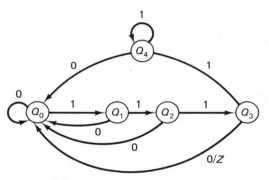

Figure 4-8

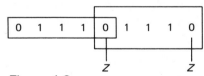

Figure 4-9

The state diagram assumes an initial state Q_0. Figure 4-8 shows the state diagram. Note that this state interpretation allows for the overlapping of input sequences, as shown in figure 4-9.

If, however, overlapping is not allowed, then the sequence in figure 4-10 defines the problem statement. The state diagram is then altered to the configuration in figure 4-11.

Figure 4-10

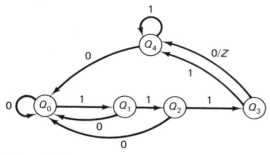

Figure 4-11

4.3 SEQUENTIAL LOGIC SYNTHESIS

The synthesis of a sequential logic circuit follows the procedure in figure 4-12. The process of going from the state diagram to the final logic circuit uses six steps that involve algorithmic techniques developed by D. Huffman. Each step will be demonstrated by a simple sequential circuit problem.

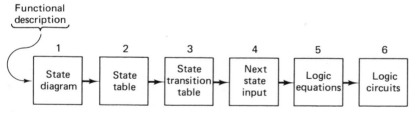

Figure 4-12 Synthesis of Sequential Logic

EXAMPLE 4.3

A clocked sequential circuit generates a clocked output whenever two or more adjacent ones occur at the input.

1. The *state diagram* for this example requires two states: (a) Q_0 which "remembers" that a zero input occurred. As long as the inputs are 0 the Q_0 state will be maintained. (b) Q_1, which remembers that the first 1 input has occurred after a 0 input. If any additional ones occur, then the

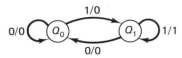

Figure 4-13   State Diagram

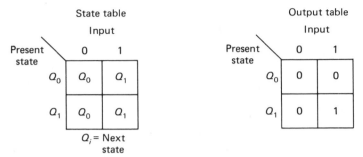

Figure 4-14   State Table and Output Table

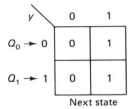

Figure 4-15   Transition Table

Q_1 state is maintained and an output is generated. Otherwise, a 0 input will cause a transition to the Q_0 state. The state diagram is shown in figure 4-13.

2. The *state table* is obtained directly from the state diagram. In fact, it is simply another representation of the same description. The output table also follows in the same manner (figure 4-14).

3. In the *transition table*, the states Q_i are assigned binary values. The selection process is somewhat arbitrary. In this example, as there are only two states, it is quite convenient to use the two Q_i subscripts as the assigned binary values (figure 4-15).

   Note that it only requires one flip-flop (y) to describe two states Q_0 and Q_1 (figure 4-16).

   In a four-state problem, two flip-flops would be used with the assignment suggested in figure 4-17.

4. The *next state input* table depends on the types of flip-flop that will be used to implement the state table. In this particular case, a D flip-flop is quite applicable to the problem, since the D flip-flop requires that the

State	Flip-flop
Q_0	$\bar{y}$
Q_1	y

Figure 4-16   Two-State Flip-Flop Assignment

States	Flip-flop	
	y_1	y_0
Q_0	0	0
Q_1	0	1
Q_2	1	0
Q_3	1	1

Figure 4-17   Four-State Flip-Flop Assignment

State change	D Input
$y(n) \longrightarrow y(n+1)$	D
$0 \longrightarrow 0$	0
$0 \longrightarrow 1$	1
$1 \longrightarrow 0$	0
$1 \longrightarrow 1$	1

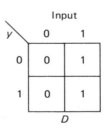

Figure 4-18   Next State Input for D Flip-Flop

next state follows the input. Thus, the next state table is the same as the state transition table (figure 4-18). The output table is shown in figure 4-19, in which Z can be expressed in terms of y.

5. From the tables, which are now in a Karnaugh map format, the *logic equations* can be obtained:

$$D = I$$

$$Z = I \cdot y$$

6. The final *logic circuit* now becomes an implementation of the logic equation (figure 4-20).

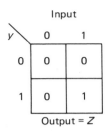

Figure 4-19   Output Table

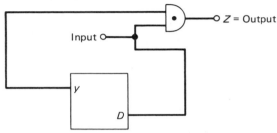

Figure 4-20   Logic Circuit

The entire process can now be summarized by placing the results in the context of figure 4-21.

EXAMPLE 4.4

Obtain the logic circuit for the functional description given in the previous example, using *SR*, *JK*, and τ flip-flops. The state transition table will be the same in all cases, so it will be used as the starting point (figure 4-22).

1. For the *SR* flip-flop, the state change table will give the conditions for generating the next state inputs (figures 4-23, 4-24, and 4-25).
2. For the *JK* flip-flop, the state change table (figure 4-26) will initiate the *JK* circuit synthesis shown in figures 4-27 and 4-28.
3. For the τ flip-flop, the state change table is again used as a starting point (see figures 4-29, 4-30, and 4-31).

EXAMPLE 4.5

Using *JK* flip-flops, synthesize a logic circuit that will give an output whenever an input sequence (100) occurs. The sequence will always be preceded by a 0.

1. *State diagram* (figure 4-32).
2. *State table* (figure 4-33).
3. *State transition table* (figure 4-34).

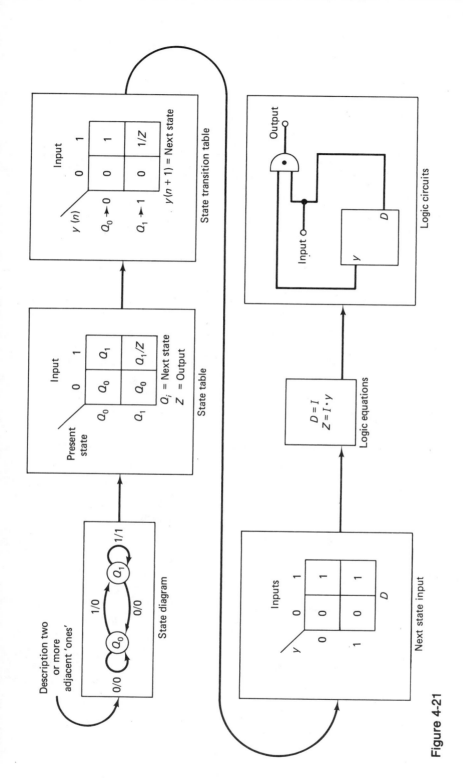

Figure 4-21

$y(n)$ \ Input	0	1
0	0	1
1	0	1

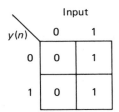

Figure 4-22 State Transition Table

State change $y(n) \longrightarrow y(n+1)$	SR Inputs SR
$0 \longrightarrow 0$	$0 \quad \phi$
$0 \longrightarrow 1$	$1 \quad 0$
$1 \longrightarrow 0$	$0 \quad 1$
$1 \longrightarrow 1$	$\phi \quad 0$

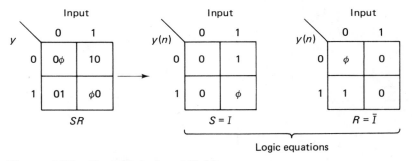

Figure 4-23 *SR* Flip-Flop State Change Table

SR:

y \ Input	0	1
0	0ϕ	10
1	01	$\phi 0$

$\longrightarrow$

$S = I$:

$y(n)$ \ Input	0	1
0	0	1
1	0	ϕ

$R = \bar{I}$:

$y(n)$ \ Input	0	1
0	ϕ	0
1	1	0

Logic equations

Figure 4-24 Next State Input Table

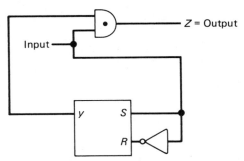

Figure 4-25 Logic Circuit

State change	JK Input
$y(n) \longrightarrow y(n+1)$	JK
$0 \longrightarrow 0$	0ϕ
$0 \longrightarrow 1$	1ϕ
$1 \longrightarrow 0$	$\phi 1$
$1 \longrightarrow 1$	$\phi 0$

Figure 4-26 JK Flip-Flop State Change Table

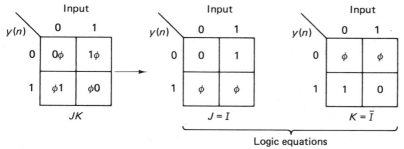

Figure 4-27   Next State Input Table

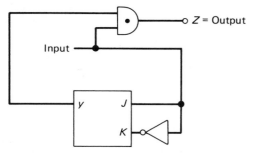

Figure 4-28   Logic Circuit

State change	τ Input
$y(n) \longrightarrow y(n+1)$	τ
0 0	0
0 1	1
1 0	1
1 1	0

Figure 4-29 τ Flip-Flop State Change Table

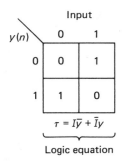

$$\tau = I\bar{y} + \bar{I}y$$

Logic equation

Figure 4-30   Next State Input Table

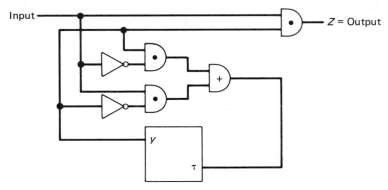

Figure 4-31   Logic Circuit

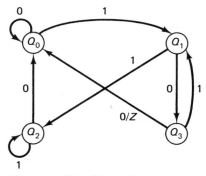

Figure 4-32   State Diagram

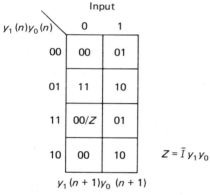

Figure 4-33   State Table

Input

$y_1(n)y_0(n)$

	0	1
00	00	01
01	11	10
11	00/Z	01
10	00	10

$Z = \bar{I}\,y_1 y_0$

$y_1(n+1)y_0(n+1)$

Figure 4-34   State Transition Table

4. *JK flip-flop next state inputs* (figure 4-35).
5. *Logic equations* (figure 4-36).

$$J_1 = y_0 + y_1$$
$$K_1 = \bar{I} + I y_0$$
$$J_0 = I \bar{y}_1$$
$$K_0 = \bar{I} y_1 + I \bar{y}_1$$

EXAMPLE 4.6

Synthesize a clocked sequential circuit that generates a clocked output when three or more ones follow a zero. Show implementations using:

1. *D* flip-flops
2. *SR* flip-flops
3. *JK* flip-flops
4. Toggle flip-flops.

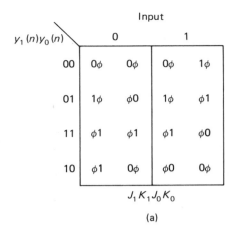

(a)

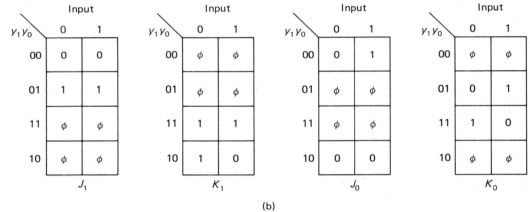

(b)

Figure 4-35 *JK* Flip-Flop Next State Inputs

Step 1: State Diagram

The *state diagram* in figure 4-37 requires a separate state to "remember" each step in the number of ones. As long as the sequence is not broken, it will remain in Q_3 and continue to generate an output.

Step 2: State Table

The state table in figure 4-38 is a direct transformation from the state diagram. Note that the outputs (Z) are incorporated into the table.

Step 3: Transition Table

The state assignments are made in the transition table in figure 4-39. For convenience, the binary equivalent of the Q_i subscripts are used. The

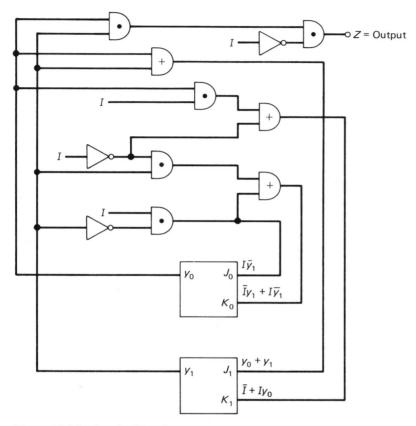

Figure 4-36   Logic Circut

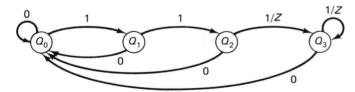

Figure 4-37   State Diagram

output table uses the same format as the table for $Q(n+1)$, except that values of Z are assigned.

Step 4: Next State Inputs and Equations

The next state inputs can be formed by first separating the transition table for each flip-flop, as in figure 4-40. From these, the next state inputs are obtained for each flip-flop type.

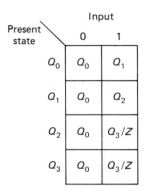

Figure 4-38 Next State Table

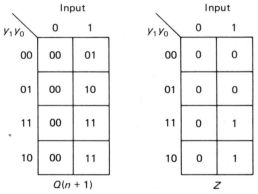

Figure 4-39 Transition Table and Output Table

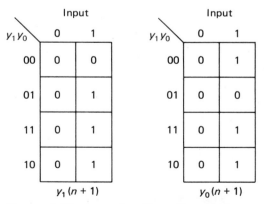

Figure 4-40 y_1 and y_0 Transition Tables

1. *D flip-flop*. The D flip-flop inputs are identical to the $Q_i(n+1)$ table so these can be used directly. Thus,

$$D_1 = I(y_1 + y_0)$$

$$D_0 = I(y_1 + \bar{y}_0)$$

2. *SR flip-flop*. For the SR flip-flop, the state changes from $y_i(n)$ to $y_i(n+1)$ will determine the SR valuations, as in figure 4-41.

    The equations are obtained from the maps.

$$S_1 = Iy_0 \quad R_1 = \bar{I}$$

$$S_0 = I\bar{y}_0 \quad R_0 = \bar{I} + \bar{y}_1 y_0$$

3. *JK flip-flop*. The JK flip-flop allows more optional conditions for the state transitions (figure 4-42), so that the final equations are somewhat simpler.

    From the maps, the equations are

$$J_1 = Iy_0 \quad K_1 = \bar{I}$$

$$J_0 = I \quad K_0 = \bar{I} + \bar{y}_1$$

4. *Toggle flip-flop*. The toggle flip-flop inputs are implemented by following the state transitions listed in figure 4-43.

    The τ equations are

$$\tau_1 = \bar{I}y_1 + I\bar{y}_1 y_0$$

$$\tau_0 = I(\bar{y}_0 + \bar{y}_1) + \bar{I}y_0$$

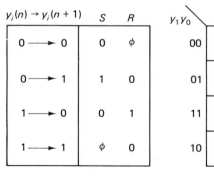
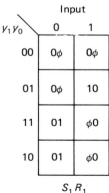
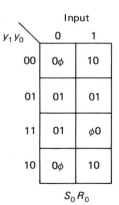

Figure 4-41   SR Flip-Flop Next State Inputs

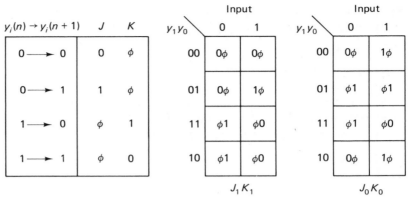

Figure 4-42   JK Flip-Flop Next State Inputs

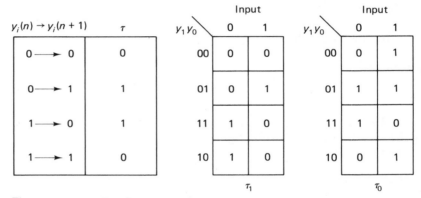

Figure 4-43 τ Flip-Flop Next State Inputs

4.4 LEVEL OUTPUT CLOCKED SEQUENTIAL

As shown earlier, a counter is a good example of a simplified level output. A more general type of level output occurs when one or more specific states are used as output states. The remaining states are used conventionally as part of the state-sequencing process. The following example is a comparison of a clocked output and a level (or state) output for identical functional descriptions.

EXAMPLE 4.7

For a clocked sequential circuit with two inputs xw, the sequence $xw = 10$ followed by $xw = 01$ will generate an output Z. Essentially, the sequence is

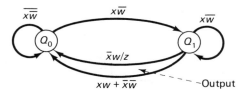

Figure 4-44   State Diagram for Clocked Output

x without w, followed by w without x—that is

$$x:\ 0\ 0\ 1\ \ 1\ 0\ \ 0\ 1\ 0$$

$$w:\ 0\ 1\ 0\ \ 0\ 1\ \ 0\ 0\ 1$$
$$\underbrace{\qquad}_{Z}\ \ \underbrace{\qquad}_{Z}$$

Show the state diagram and the timing diagram for (1) a clocked output and (2) a level output.

1. For a clocked output Z, the state and timing diagrams are shown in figures 4-44 and 4-45.
2. For a level output, the state and timing diagrams are shown in figures 4-46 and 4-47.

   For case 2, when the present state is Q_1, which recognized an x alone, the occurrence of a w alone will require an *additional* state (Q_2), which is used as the *level output*. Thus, even for the same problem, a state diagram for level outputs will be visibly different from that for a clocked output.
   A comparison of (1) and (2) shows how a choice is available for when to generate the output. The clocked output in (1) (figure 4-45) is really a level that can be inputed to another operation at the $n+2$ clock time. The level output in (2) (figure 4-47) is present during the *entire interval* between $n+2$ and $n+3$. Since it is being "remembered" by Q_2, it is available for clocking at $n+3$.

4.5 PULSED SEQUENTIAL CIRCUITS

In our definition of sequential circuits, the states are always levels. This is a convenience, because these levels are memory conditions that keep track of the place in a sequence. Although inputs have also been defined as levels, there is a useful group of sequential circuits in which this is not the case. These are pulsed input circuits. There are two differences between

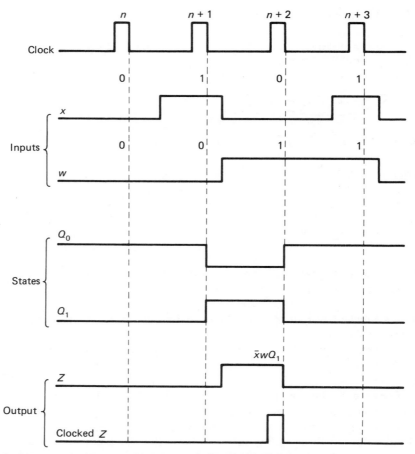

Figure 4-45   Timing Diagram for Clocked Output

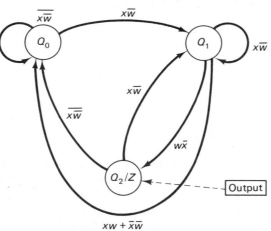

Figure 4-46   State Diagram for Level Output

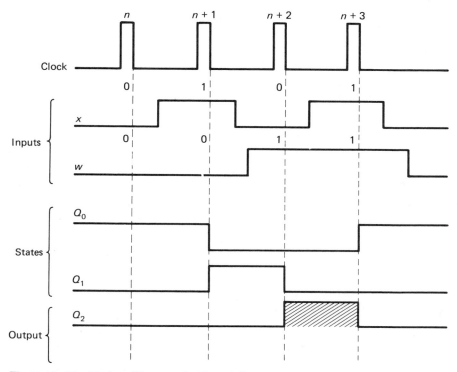

Figure 4-47   Timing Diagram for Level Output

pulsed and level inputs:

1. Pulsed inputs require that only *one* input can occur at a time, because the occurrence of two simultaneous pulsed inputs is physically quite difficult to accomplish.

2. Also, the pulse is in effect *its own clock*, so that pulsed input circuits are not necessarily synchronous.

For a pulsed input, which may typically be only 25 nanoseconds wide, there is the problem of making it occur simultaneously with other pulses. In figure 4-48, pulse A is modified by some logic circuits that have built-in delays of 1 to 10 nanoseconds each. It is possible that this delay could build up to at least the width of A. Therefore, although A and B do occur simultaneously, A' now occurs *later* than A, so that a coincidence of B and A' is impossible.

Pulsed sequential circuits can be classified according to the form of their output. When a pulsed output is formed it is called a *Mealy circuit*, and a level output is a *Moore circuit*, each named after the men who published some of the earliest papers on the subject.

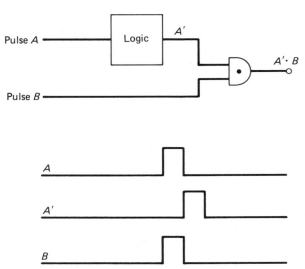

Figure 4-48

Table 4-1   Sequential Circuit Classification

	Inputs	States (Q)	Outputs
Clocked sequential:			
Pulse output	Level	Level	Pulse $= f(Q, \text{Input}, \text{Clock})$
Level output	Level	Level	Level $= f(Q)$
Pulsed sequential:			
Pulse output	Pulse	Level	Pulse $= f(Q, \text{Input})$
Level output	Pulse	Level	Level $= f(Q)$

Table 4-1 shows where levels and pulses are used for different types of sequential circuits.

Pulsed sequential logic is synthesized in the same manner as clocked sequential. The places where differences occur can be shown by examples.

EXAMPLE 4.8

The same description as in example 4-7 will be used. An input pulse sequence is to be detected in which x occurs alone, followed by w alone. An output will be generated every time this sequence is completed.

Show the state and timing diagrams for (1) a pulsed output and (2) a level output.

1. Figures 4-49 and 4-50 show the diagrams for a pulse output.
2. The state and timing diagrams for a level output are shown in figures 4-51 and 4-52.

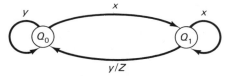

Figure 4-49   State Diagram for Pulse Output

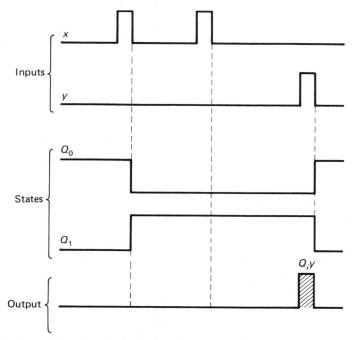

Figure 4-50   Timing Diagram for Pulse Output

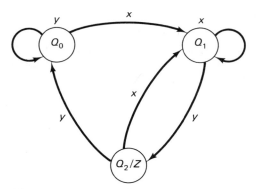

Figure 4-51   State Diagram for Level Output

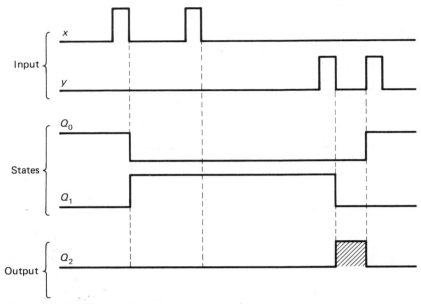

Figure 4-52   Timing Diagram for Level Output

Because the circuit is formed by the occurrence of inputs, the Q_2 output state will generate an output *until* a new input changes the state conditions.

EXAMPLE 4.9

Obtain the logic implementation for a circuit which generates a pulsed output whenever a pulsed input sequence *xxxw* occurs.

1. The state diagram (figure 4-53).
2. The state table (figure 4-54).

    Note that for pulsed inputs there is only one condition for each input, the presence of the pulse. The input table comparing level inputs with pulse inputs is given as table 4-2.

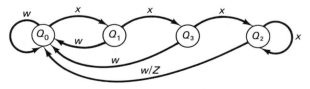

Figure 4-53

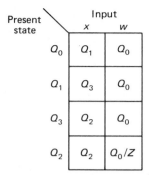

Figure 4-54   State Table

Table 4-2   Level and Pulse Input Comparison

| | Inputs | |
Level		Pulse
$\bar{x}\bar{w}$		Does not occur, since there is no clock
$\bar{x}w$		w
$x\bar{w}$		x
xw		Not allowed

3. The transition table (figure 4-55).
4. The next inputs for a τ flip-flop (figure 4-56).
5. The logic equations:

$$\tau_1 = x\bar{y}_1 y_0 + wy_1$$

$$\tau_0 = x(\bar{y}_1\bar{y}_0 + y_1 y_0) + wy_0$$

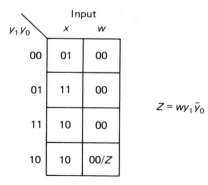

$$Z = wy_1\bar{y}_0$$

Figure 4-55   Transition Table

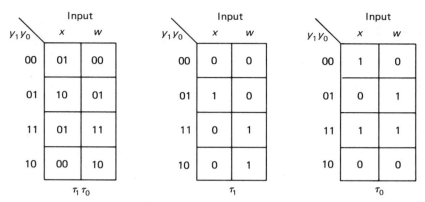

$y_1 y_0$	Input x	Input w
00	01	00
01	10	01
11	01	11
10	00	10

$\tau_1 \tau_0$

$y_1 y_0$	Input x	Input w
00	0	0
01	1	0
11	0	1
10	0	1

τ_1

$y_1 y_0$	Input x	Input w
00	1	0
01	0	1
11	1	1
10	0	0

τ_0

Figure 4-56   Next State Inputs

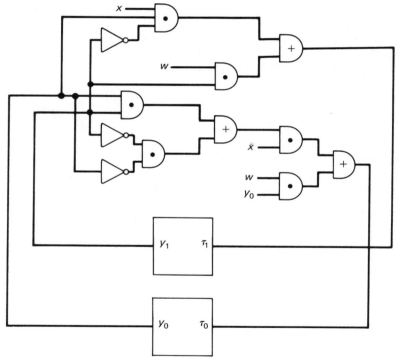

Figure 4-57   Logic Circuit

Note that the $y_1 y_0$ term *cannot* be used. It is necessary to have an input pulsed term in each expression because the circuit is being "clocked" by the inputs.

6. *Logic circuit* (figure 4-57).

The logic diagram has been shown in a functional manner, which ignores the means of clocking the flip-flop. For an actual implementation, one method is to feed the toggle condition into the clock input of the flip-flop and a logic 1 into the τ input. This result gives the same effect as in a clocked circuit.

4.6 EQUIVALENT FLIP-FLOPS

One of the curiosities of binary storage elements is the variation of input types used for flip-flops. A particular problem is to determine how to take a flip-flop with one input form and implement it with another flip-flop type. The more obvious method is to return to the original state table and redo the procedure for obtaining the next state inputs. However, this is really not necessary. By capitalizing on the understanding of sequential logic synthesis, an "equivalent" flip-flop can be generated. The approach is as follows:

Problem: To implement an "equivalent" JK flip-flop by using a τ flip-flop (figure 4-58).

Solution: Obtain the *logic* for the "equivalent" JK flip-flop (figure 4-59). The philosophy of "equivalent" flip-flops is to

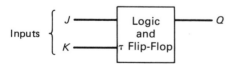

Figure 4-58

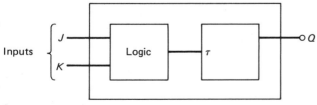

Figure 4-59   An "Equivalent" JK Flip-Flop

1. Form the state transition table, in which the table *inputs* are the *JK* inputs to the given flip-flop. That is, given a *JK*, set up the table for

$$Q(n+1) = f(Q(n), J, K)$$

2. *Implement* the next state *input* table for the desired implementing flip-flop input (τ). That is, to implement with a τ flip-flop, set up the table for

$$\tau = f(Q(n), J, K)$$

This approach is illustrated by example 4-10.

EXAMPLE 4.10

Given a circuit in which all equations are written for *JK* flip-flops, generate an "equivalent" *JK*, using *SR*, τ, and *D* flip-flops.

The process is started by first obtaining the $Q(n+1)$ state transition table for the *JK* flip-flop (figure 4-60).

1. The "equivalent" *JK*, using an *SR*, has the structure shown in figure 4-61.

To obtain the "equivalent" flip-flop, form an *SR* next state input table for $Q(n+1)$ (figure 4-62). This results in the following equations as a function of *JK* inputs:

$$S = J\overline{Q}$$
$$R = KQ$$

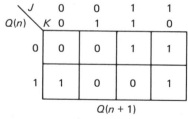

Figure 4-60   State Transition Table

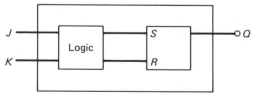

Figure 4-61   An "Equivalent" *JK* Using *SR*

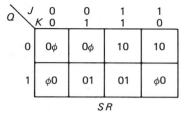

Figure 4-62   Next State Input Table

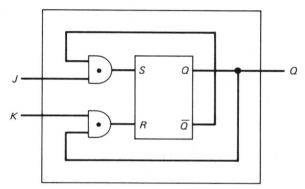

Figure 4-63   "Equivalent" *JK* Implemented with *SR*

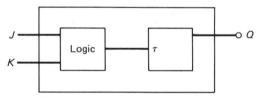

Figure 4-64   An "Equivalent" *JK* Using τ

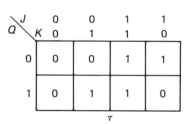

Figure 4-65   Next State Input Table

From these the logic diagram in figure 4-63 is formed. This shows in a systematic manner how an "equivalent" *JK* flip-flop can be constructed from an *SR*.

2. For an "equivalent" *JK* using τ inputs (figure 4-64), the procedure is repeated by using a τ next state table (figure 4-65). The *logic equation* is:

$$\tau = J\overline{Q} + KQ$$

The "equivalent" flip-flop logic is shown in figure 4-66.

3. The same procedure is used to form a *D* "equivalent" *JK* (figure 4-67).

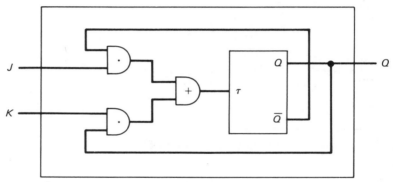

Figure 4-66   "Equivalent" *JK* Implemented with τ

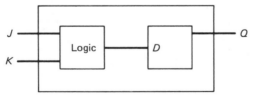

Figure 4-67   An "Equivalent" *JK* Using *D*

Q \ JK	0 0	0 1	1 1	1 0
0	0	0	1	1
1	1	0	0	1

D

Figure 4-68   Next State Input Table

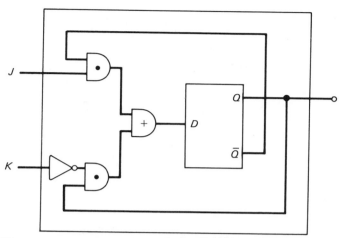

Figure 4-69 "Equivalent" *JK* Implemented with *D*

The *D* next state input table is formed in figure 4-68. The logic equation for *D* is

$$D = J\overline{Q} + \overline{K}Q$$

Figure 4-69 shows the "equivalent" flip-flop logic.

EXAMPLE 4.11

In example 4.6, the sequential circuit was synthesized for a *D*, *SR*, *JK*, and toggle flip-flop. Taking the equations developed for D_1,

$$D_1 = I(y_1 + y_0)$$

by using "equivalent" *D* flip-flops, obtain the equations for S_1, R_1, $J_1 K_1$, and τ_1.

The procedure requires that the equation for the "equivalent" *D* flip-flops be obtained.

The state table for the *D* flip-flop is shown in figure 4-70. From this, the next input tables (figure 4-71) and the resultant equations are obtained.

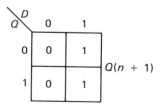

Figure 4-70 Next State Table

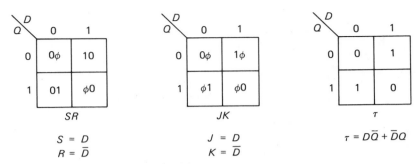

$$S = D$$
$$R = \bar{D}$$

$$J = D$$
$$K = \bar{D}$$

$$\tau = D\bar{Q} + \bar{D}Q$$

Figure 4-71   Next State Tables

Taking the equation for D_1

$$D_1 = I(y_1 + y_0)$$

This is substituted into the appropriate equation:

1. $S_1 = I(y_1 + y_0)$
   $R_1 = \bar{I} + (\bar{y}_1 \bar{y}_0)$
2. $J_1 = S_1$
   $K_1 = R_1$
3. $\tau_1 = I(y_1 + y_0)\bar{y}_1 + \overline{I(y_1 + y_0)}y_1$
   $= I\bar{y}_1 y_0 + \bar{I}y_1$

These results are logically correct and equivalent to the preceding results. Redundant terms appear because of the use of the "unspecified" terms in the map.

PROBLEMS

1. A clocked sequential circuit with a clocked output recognizes an input sequence of at least 8 ones in a row.
   (a) Show the state diagram.
   (b) Generate the logic circuits to implement this using τ, D, SR, and JK flip-flops.

2. Repeat problem 1 with pulsed inputs.

3. A clocked sequential circuit has two inputs, X and Y. Whenever a sequence of two $\bar{X}Y$'s followed by two $X\bar{Y}$'s occurs, a clocked output will be generated.
   (a) Show the state diagram.
   (b) Generate the logic circuits using τ, D, SR, and JK flip-flops.

4. Using the D equations for problem 3, obtain the τ, SR, and JK equations by using equivalent flip-flops.

5. Repeat problem 3 for a Mealy circuit (pulsed input, pulsed output).

6. Repeat problem 3 for a Moore circuit (pulsed input, level output).

Bibliography

Chapter 1

Babbage, R. H. "The Work of Charles Babbage." In *Annals of the Computation Laboratory of Harvard University*, vol. 16 (pp. 13–22). Cambridge, Mass.: Harvard University Press, 1948.

Bell, C. G.; Grason, J.; and Newell, A. *Designing Computers and Digital Systems*. Maynard, Mass.: Digital Press, 1972.

Blakeslee, T. R. *Digital Design with Standard MSI and LSI*. New York: Wiley, 1974.

Burks, A. W.; Goldstine, H. H.; and von Neumann, J. *Preliminary Discussion of the Logical Design of an Electronic Computing Instrument*, part 1, vol. 1. Princeton: Institute for Advanced Study, 1946.

Carr, William N., and Mize, Jack P. *MOS/LSI Design and Application*. Texas Instruments Electronic Series. New York: McGraw-Hill, 1972.

Digital Equipment Corp. *LSI-11 Microcomputer*. Maynard, Mass.: DEC, 1975.

Goldstine, H. H. *The Computer from Pascal to von Neumann*. Princeton, N.J.: Princeton University Press, 1972.

IBM. *The Computer Age, the Evolution of IBM Computers*. Armonk, New York: IBM, 1976.

Korn, G. A. *Minicomputers for Engineers and Scientists*. New York: McGraw-Hill, 1973.

RCA. *COS/MOS Integrated Circuits Manual*. Somerville, N.J.: RCA, 1972.

Schoeffler, J. D., and Temple, R. H., eds. *Minicomputers: Hardware, Software, and Applications*. New York: IEEE Press, 1972.

Shannon, C. "A Symbolic Analysis of Relay and Switching Circuits." *Trans. AIEE* 57 (1938): 713–23.

Smith, D. E. *History of Mathematics* (2 vols.). New York: Dover, 1958.

Texas Instruments, Engineering Staff. *The Integrated Circuits Catalog for Design Engineers*. Dallas: Texas Instruments, n.d.

Wiener, N. *Cybernetics, or Control and Communication in the Animal and the Machine*. New York: Wiley, 1948.

Zuse, K. "German Computer Activities." In *Computers and Their Future*, pp. 6/3–6/17. Llandudno: Richard Williams and Partners, 1970.

Chapter 2

Birkhoff, G., and S. MacLane. *Survey of Modern Algebra*. 3rd ed. New York: Macmillan, 1965.

Blakeslee, T. R. *Digital Design with Standard MSI and LSI*. New York: Wiley, 1975.

Boole, George. *An Investigation of the Laws of Thought*. New York: Dover Publications, 1954.

Boole, G. *The Mathematical Analysis of Logic*. Cambridge, 1847.

Boole, G. *An Investigation of the Laws of Thought on Which Are Founded the Mathematical Theories of Logic and Probabilities*. London, 1854.

Caldwell, S. H. *Switching Circuits and Logical Design*. New York: Wiley, 1960.

Chu, Y. *Digital Computer Design Fundamentals*. New York: McGraw-Hill, 1962.

Flores, I. *Logic of Computer Arithmetic*. Englewood Cliffs, N.J. Prentice-Hall, 1963.

Hill, F. J., and Peterson, G. R. *Introduction to Switching Theory and Logical Design*. New York: Wiley, 1968.

Huntington, E. V. "Sets of Independent Postulates for the Algebra of Logic." *Trans. American Math. Soc.* 5 (1904): 288–309.

Karnaugh, M. "The Map Method for Synthesis of Combinational Logic Circuits." *Trans. AIEE* 72, pt. 1 (1953): 593–98.

Logic Products Group. *Logic Handbook*. Maynard, Mass.: Digital Press, 1973.

McCluskey, E. J. *Introduction to the Theory of Switching Circuits*. New York: McGraw-Hill, 1965.

Millman, J., and Taub, H. *Pulse, Digital, and Switching Waveforms*. New York: McGraw-Hill, 1965.

Morris, Robert L., and Miller, J. R., eds. *Designing with TTL Integrated Circuits*. N.Y., Texas Instruments Electronic Series. New York: McGraw-Hill, 1972.

Quine, W. V. *Mathematical Logic*. Cambridge, Mass.: Harvard University Press, 1955.

Sheffer, H. M. "A Set of Five Independent Postulates for Boolean Algebras, with Applications to Logical Constants." *Trans. American Math. Soc.* 14 (1913): 481–88.

TTL Applications Handbook. Mountain View, Calif.: Fairchild Semiconductor, 1972.

The TTL Data Book for Design Engineers. Dallas, Texas: Texas Instruments, Inc., 1973.

Veitch, E. W. "A Chart Method for Simplifying Truth Functions." *Proc. ACM, Pittsburgh, Pa.* (May 2, 3, 1952): 127–33.

Chapter 3

Eccles, W. H., and Jordan, F. W. "A Trigger Relay Utilizing Three-Electrode Thermionic Vacuum Tubes." *The Radio Review* 1 (1919): 143–46.

Hellerman, H. *Digital Computer System Principles*. New York: McGraw-Hill, 1973.

Rhyne, V. T. *Fundamentals of Digital Systems Design*. Englewood Cliffs, N.J.: Prentice-Hall, 1973.

Sobel, H. S. *Introduction to Digital Computer Design*. Reading, Mass.: Addison-Wesley, 1970.

Chapter 4

Caldwell, S. H. *Switching Circuits and Logical Design*. New York: Wiley, 1958.

Dolotta, T. A., and McClusky, E. J. "The Coding of Internal States of Sequential Circuits." *IEEE Trans. On Electronic Computers*, EC-13, no. 5 (October, 1964): 549–62.

Gill, Arthur. *Introduction to the Theory of Finite State Machines*. New York: McGraw-Hill, 1962.

Hartmanis, J. "On the State Assignment Problem for Sequential Machines, I." *IRE Trans. on Electronic Computers*, EC-10, no. 2 (June, 1961): 157–65.

Hartmanis, J., and Stearns, R. E. *Algebraic Structure Theory of Sequential Machines*. Englewood Cliffs, N.J.: Prentice-Hall, 1966.

Hennie. F. C. *Finite-State Models for Logical Machines*. New York: Wiley, 1968.

Huffman, D. A. "The Synthesis of Sequential Switching Circuits." *J. Franklin Inst.* 257, no. 3, 161–90, and no. 4, 275–303 (March-April, 1954).

Huffman, D. A. "A Study of the Memory Requirements of Sequential Switching Circuits." *Technical Report No. 293*. Research Laboratory of Electronics, M.I.T., April 1955.

Karp, R. M. "Some Techniques of State Assignment for Synchronous Sequential Machines." *IEEE Trans. of Electronic Computers*, EC-13, no. 5 (October, 1964): 507–18.

McCluskey, E. J. "Fundamental Mode and Pulse Mode Sequential Circuits." *Proc. IFIP Congress 1962*. Amsterdam: North Holland Publ. Co., 1963.

Mealy, G. H. "A Method for Synthesizing Sequential Circuits." *Bell System Tech. J.* 34, no. 5 (September, 1955): 1045–80.

Moore, E. F. "Gedanken Experiments on Sequential Machines." In *Automata Studies*, edited by C. E. Shannon and J. McCarthy. Princeton, N.J.: Princeton Univ. Press, 1956.

Moore, E. F. *Sequential Machines, Selected Papers*. Reading, Mass.: Addison-Wesley, 1964.

Paull, M. C., and Unger S. H. "Minimizing the Number of States in Incompletely Specified Sequential Switching Functions." *IRE Trans. on Electronic Computers*, EC-8, no. 3 (September, 1959): 356–57.

Stearns, R. E., and Hartmanis, J. "On the State Assignment Problem for Sequential Machines, II." *IRE Trans. on Electronic Computers*, EC-10, no. 4 (December, 1961): 593–603.

Index

Italic page numbers designate illustrations.